Lenses
for
Design

Josh Owen

RIT Press
Rochester, New York

**Lenses
for
Design**

Josh Owen
www.joshowen.com

First Printing September 2016

ISBN 978-1-939125-33-0 (print)
ISBN 978-1-939125-34-7 (ebook)

Published and distributed by
RIT Press
90 Lomb Memorial Drive
Rochester, NY 14623
ritpress.rit.edu

Printed in the USA

Written by Josh Owen
Book design by Bruce Ian Meader
and Josh Owen

Library of Congress
Cataloging-in-Publication Data

Names: Owen, Josh, 1970- author
Title: Lenses for design/Josh Owen
Description: Rochester, New York: RIT Press, 2016
Includes index
Identifiers: LCCN 2016031390 (print)
LCCN 2016031855 (ebook)
ISBN 9781939125330 (hardcover: alk. paper)
ISBN 9781939125347 (ebook)
Subjects: LCSH: Design—Philosophy | Owen, Josh
1970—Aesthetics
Classification: LCC NK1505 .094 2016 (print)
LCC NK1505 (ebook) | DDC 745.4—dc23
LC record available at https://lccn.loc.gov/2016031390

Contents

Dedication

I dedicate this book to my son, Jasper, and daughter, Saskia, to whom I often ask, hoping to discourage complaining, "If there is a problem, what do we do?"

"We find a solution, Dad!"

My intent in asking is to encourage them to take a step back from a problem and learn from the process of developing and considering a plausible resolution.

Learning to see clearly by adjusting perspective is likewise a process of discovering a set of meaningful actions to address one's happiness while reducing the chance of encountering the problem again.

In Search of the
Essence of Things

Mathias Schwartz-Clauss

Curator
Directeur, Domaine de Boisbuchet

Josh Owen's design is like Josh Owen himself—
a human, esthetical, and spiritual experience.
The person and his creations are concentrated, clear,
reasonable, and optimistic.

Explaining the origins of his career choice, Owen
reflects on his father's archeological excavations,
in which he participated as a boy. He remembers
himself as a student drawing sculptures in Rome,
and tells of his studies in anthropology. This early
training quite obviously showed him the way to
design as much as characterized his current work
process: Owen examines our cultural heritage,
explores the human condition, and carefully builds
on the shoulders of giants. Consequently, he backs
up his practice through constant reflection with a
dual purpose—for the systematic documentation and
analysis of his own designs and conveying know-how
in his role as a passionate teacher. "All good design
is incrementalism," says this professed advocate of
details. While emphasizing design's significance for
language and function, Owen explains how the ways
in which we navigate the world are rapidly changing.
In view of the environmental and social challenges of
today's globalization, he sets high priorities for clear
communication—and the questions his designs ask are
fundamentally moral. They are clear-cut; not interested
in what we can do but what we should do in order to
move humanity forward rather than backward.

Enlightened Lessons

Scott Klinker

3-D Designer-in-Residence
Cranbrook Academy of Art

Design, as a practice, is hard to understand. Located somewhere between Art and Science, Design helps people make sense of the material world that surrounds us. How a designer actually accomplishes this "making sense" is even harder to explain, let alone teach. A designer spends years, even decades, observing culture, looking for patterns, trying experiments, failing, learning, and trying again in an endless crawl toward a cultural sensibility that may finally enable him to create "things" that contribute something to the world. It requires a tireless optimist who is equal parts maker, thinker, philosopher, artist, entrepreneur, social scientist, engineer, critic, and collaborator. In addition to this mix, it takes someone with empathy for others who honestly wants to improve things.

A small minority of designers embodies all of these qualities, and even fewer do so with the Zen-like calm of Josh Owen. Even at his young age, Josh is reaching sage status—able to translate his wisdom into useful principles to enlighten young designers. It's this idea of enlightenment that separates a mere instructor from a gifted teacher. An instructor might explain the techniques of design, but a real teacher will impart the ability to think and feel like a designer. Josh's lenses for design are intended to do just that—enlighten young designers to see the world through the eyes of a designer. A noble goal and a tall order, too.

These lenses for design are more than design instruction. They are principles to live by or, as the concept implies, principles to see by: "If you look through this lens, then you can see like a designer." It's clear even from the title of this book that Josh is interested in doing more than just teaching a process of design: he wants to share a vision.

But his teaching doesn't stop at abstract theory or principles. Josh "walks the talk" right out onto the street. Whether it's demonstrating his ideas in case studies from his own industry projects with collaborators around the world or directing his real-world "Meta-Projects" that allow students to engage directly with industry sponsors, Josh knows how to apply ideas and make them tangible. His ability to lead by example often is missing in education today. The old adage, "Those who can't do, teach" is too often true, but Josh is a bright exception to this rule—building a practice that seamlessly integrates award-winning projects and educational leadership.

Real-world application in design education is not always done right. Too many sponsored projects that only judge the commercial potential of a design can stunt the growth of a young designer's imagination and vision. Design in fact is not only a commercial pursuit, but also a way of looking critically and propositionally at what our collective future could be. It's a way of testing our values and giving them form. It asks, "What if my world looked like this?" Josh knows how to build a project that refuses to sacrifice educational goals for commercial ones. Whether his students are questioning new behaviors in the workplace for Herman Miller or designing new toys for Areaware, his Meta-Projects always have cultural research as their ultimate goal.

This balance between theory and practice makes Josh both a gifted designer and a gifted teacher, with the bigness of heart to know the difference between mere instruction and enlightening lessons. It takes a real designer to teach us how to see like one.

Preface

While designing objects and teaching design this last decade, I have been collecting design lessons. These lessons stem from my professional experiences in the design industry and my interactions with clients, colleagues, and students. Many of the lessons have made their way back to the classroom and to subsequent client projects.

Initially, I thought I might put together a series of lessons as lectures or discussions on specific topics. But I learned from my students and clients that both were particularly interested in understanding how my, perhaps idiosyncratic, "ways of seeing" influence my teaching and design process.

Encouraged by their interest, I decided to try to define and explain what I hereafter refer to as lenses for design. It is my hope that these lenses will provide some new perspectives to help others move their own ideas forward.

Introduction

Josh Owen

At work in his design studio
Rochester, New York
2015

**Owen's vision of Design is advanced
rooted in humanist culture
spare and timeless**
Massimo Vignelli

Leather Satchel

Archetypical design
purchased from
a book vendor who
was not planning to
sell the object.

Book Bazaar
Istanbul, Turkey
1998

I do not seek, I find
Pablo Picasso

Didgeridoo

Eucalyptus branch
hollowed out by termites,
the didgeridoo is an
indigenous Australian
wind instrument developed
in northern Australia
around 1,500 years ago
and is still in widespread use
today in Australia and
around the world.

It is often described as a
natural wooden trumpet
or 'drone pipe' and is
played with continuously
vibrating lips to produce
low droning sounds using
a breathing technique
called circular breathing.

Northern Territory
Australia 2012

Nothing is simple
Common Saying

si·mon-pure \...\ ...
character impersonated by ... (1718) by Susannah Centlivre] (to ...
also : pretentiously or hypocritically pure

si·mo·ny \'sī-mə-nē, 'si-\ n [ME *symonie*, fr. AF, ... nia, fr. *Simon Magus*, Samaritan sorcerer in Acts 8: ... buying or selling of a church office or ecclesiastical preferment

si·moom \sə-'müm, sī-\ *or* si·moon \-'mün\ n [Ar *samūm*] (1790) : a hot dry violent dust-laden wind from Asian and African deserts

simp \'simp\ n (1903) : SIMPLETON

sim·pa·ti·co \sim-'pä-ti-ˌkō, -'pa-\ adj [It *simpatico* & Sp *simpático*, ul-tim. fr. L *sympathia* sympathy] (1864)   1 : AGREEABLE, LIKABLE   2 : being on the same wavelength : CONGENIAL, SYMPATHETIC

¹sim·per \'sim-pər\ vb sim·pered; sim·per·ing \-p(ə-)riŋ\ [akin to MD *zimperlijc* elegant, Dan dial. *simper* affected, coy] vi (ca. 1563) : to smile in a silly manner ~ vt : to say with a simper ⟨~ed an apology⟩ —
sim·per·er \-pər-ər\ n

²simper n (1599) : a silly smile : SMIRK

¹sim·ple \'sim-pəl\ adj sim·pler \-p(ə-)lər\; sim·plest \-p(ə-)ləst\ [ME, fr. AF, fr. ML *simplus*, alter. of L *simplic-, simplex* single, having one in-gredient, plain, fr. *sem-, sim-* one + *-plic-, -plex* -fold — more at SAME, -FOLD] (13c)   1 : free from guile : INNOCENT   2 a : free from vanity   b : free from ostentation or display ⟨a ~ outfit⟩   3 : of humble origin or modest position ⟨a ~ farmer⟩   4 a : lacking in knowledge or expertise ⟨a ~ amateur of the arts⟩   b (1) : STUPID : mentally retarded   c : not socially or culturally sophisticated : NA-IVE; *also* : CREDULOUS   5 a : SHEER, UNMIXED ⟨~ honesty⟩   b : free of secondary complications ⟨a ~ vitamin deficiency⟩   c (1) : having only one main clause and no subordinate clauses ⟨a ~ sentence⟩   (2) : of a subject or predicate : having no modifiers, complements, or objects   d : constituting a basic element : FUNDAMENTAL   e : not made up of many like units ⟨a ~ eye⟩   6 : free from elaboration or figuration ⟨a harmony⟩   7 a (1) : not subdivided into branches or leaflets ⟨a ~ stem⟩ ⟨a ~ leaf⟩   (2) : consisting of a single carpel   (3) : develop-ing from a single ovary ⟨a ~ fruit⟩   b : controlled by a single gene ⟨~ in-herited characters⟩   8 : not limited or restricted : UNCONDITIONAL ⟨~ directi-⟩   9 : readily understood or performed ⟨~   ~ obligation⟩   10 of a statistical hypothesis : s ⟨the adjustment was ~ to make⟩ ... statistical parameters — com-fying exact values for one or more statistical parameters — COMPOSITE 3 — sim·ple·ness \-pəl-nəs\ n

syn SIMPLE, FOOLISH, SILLY, FATUOUS, ASININE mean actually parently deficient in intelligence. SIMPLE implies a degree of gence inadequate to cope with anything complex or involving effort ⟨considered people *simple* who had trouble with com-FOOLISH implies the character of being or seeming unable to ment, discretion, or good sense ⟨*foolish* stunts⟩. SILLY sugge to act as a rational being esp. by ridiculous behavior ⟨the sil revelers⟩. FATUOUS implies foolishness, inanity, and disreg ity ⟨*fatuous* conspiracy theories⟩. ASININE suggests utte temptible failure to use normal rationality or perception plot⟩.   syn see in addition EASY

²simple n (14c)   1 a : a person of humble birth : COMMO very little of anybody, ~s or gentry —Virginia Woolf⟩ or credulous person : IGNORAMUS   (2) : a mentally reta a : a medicinal plant   b : a vegetable drug having only 3 : one component of a complex; *specif* : an unanalyza

simple closed curve n (1919) : a closed plane curve ...⟩ that does not intersect itself — called also Jor

simple equation n (1758) : a linear equation

simple fraction n (ca. 1728) : a fraction having who ...tor and denominator ... compare COMPLEX ... (1597) : a bone fracture that do ... are COMPOUND FRACT

Finding Simple

While curiosity is an important asset for the designer, the wisdom that emerges by developing clarity of purpose and rejecting fashion is essential for finding. Finding requires knowledge that a solution can be reached after examination or investigation. It implies a deliberate path, dedicated to a particular result.

Simplicity has always been an important human value. Perhaps today it is more important than ever. We live in a complex reality, convoluted by more streams of information than we may ever have collectively imagined possible. Our behaviors have changed, but our ability to process the impact of this change is limited. The desire to take control of change demands that we understand how to distill what is central to our existence and what is meaningful in the context of our day-to-day lives.

I have been fortunate to work with talented individuals in my professional career. Many of my partners no doubt will recount my often-uttered phrase, "Nothing is simple." A better statement might be, "Nothing is simple, but everything should aspire to be."

The job of the designer is to employ empathy in cultivating a result. Reducing the number of steps required to solve a problem can be complicated, but the effect on the recipient should be intuitive. The response to good design—"Why didn't I think of that?"— implies that the solution is so simple that it should have been obvious, and is what we often hope for in a successful outcome.

The magnifying glass repeated as an icon in this book is a useful example. At first glance, there is little to notice. The archetypal visual form is almost a cartoon. We see a circular glass, wrapped in a metal ring, supported by a faceted, tapered plastic handle. There are no notable adornments, no ornamentation. This object is a tool, not a moniker of status or an expression of an idea. But on closer observation, the glass is carefully sized, shaped, and formed to allow a range of text and imagery to be amplified by manipulating its position relative to a source material. Picking it up, one quickly realizes there is weight to the object, giving it a feeling of import. But it is not too heavy for an average person to hold. The hand naturally finds the facets on the handle that make for easy adjustments from side to side for better viewing and to maintain focus on areas of interest. It feels balanced—effortless to use. A closer look at construction reveals the thoughtfulness of the metal ring's connection to the handle. A threaded screw is split in half and bound when inserted into the shaft of the handle, pulling the lens into position. This is an object made to last, economical with as few parts as possible; each element considered and balanced for maximum effect. It seems no wonder that it fits into the landscape of my desk, looking as contemporary now as it did when it was produced nearly 80 years ago.

We learn from the magnifying glass that an object that "finds simple" is, in truth, complex. The complexity of formulation results in an expression of purity. In order to create depth and heft in minimalism, there must be the weight of thought behind an outcome. In order to achieve sophistication through simplicity, there must be a strategy involving informed and practiced restraint.

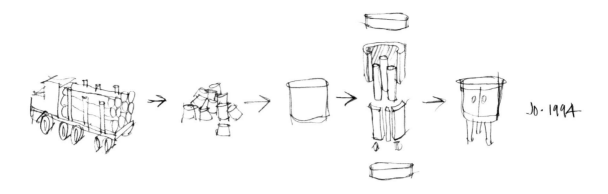

Natural Sustainability

One day while living in the wooded landscape of western New York, I watched a lumber truck rumble by, freshly loaded with tree trunks from a local logging operation. I wondered how it was possible that all the neatly trimmed and de-branched logs on the flatbed of this vehicle seemed to be exactly the same length. Was it possible that the lumber industry cultivated trees that grew to exactly the same size? Obviously there would have to be some discrepancy in overall length, no matter how close in nature and nurture they were. I visited some lumber mills with this question on my mind. Sure enough, each mill had a pile of cut-off tree ends. Here was the answer to my query. When quizzed on the fate of these "extras," the proprietors told me similar stories. Some employees cut them up for firewood or used them to make butcher-block tables. But mostly, they were piled against the woods from which they had emerged, slowly decomposing and returning to the soil to nourish the next generation of lumber. So when I asked if I could take what I could carry, the answer was always, "Sure, glad you can put them to some use."

I took what I could in the back of my second-hand Dodge Shadow, wedging in short pieces and challenging the capacity of an automobile surely not designed to carry such weight. The soaked stumps sat in my studio for a few weeks, becoming slightly less soaked before I began to operate on them.

At that time, I had not previously worked in wood. The bulk of my training had been in plaster, clay, steel, and bronze. But sometimes, ignorance breeds the most unusual of approaches. I thought of the wood in the same way that I did these other materials—for better or worse. I drew a few lines on the trunks, borrowed a chainsaw, and proceeded to cut. Working respectfully with the matter I was afforded, I schemed to remove the bare minimum of material necessary to make functional objects. From the logs' interiors I found the masses I needed for extra items, like legs or handles, and any details I needed for joinery. I built chairs, tables, and storage units to mirror the basic conditions of human existence: sitting, elevating things above the ground, and storing items away. I attempted to account for the tree trunk's movements around the concentric circular grain as the material dried out over time by fastening all parts together with pegs. I remember enjoying the way the material reacted to my plans. In some areas it rebelled by cracking. Rather than reject these imperfections, I celebrated them by highlighting the details. A good designer always pushes material to perform but respects the material's natural capacity.

When I sat down to write this book, I realized that the focus of my work always has been to make enduring choices about material, technology, usability, and semantics. More than 20 years later, a cabinet and a stool I made from that found wood remain at work in my living room, blending, just slightly, into the woodwork that surrounds them.

Developing Lenses

When I was a boy, I would collect things I found, placing them in a large wooden box in the bedroom I shared with my brother. These were not toys or things that one might imagine a child would gravitate to, but artifacts, pieces of nature, and fragments of industry. Initially I likely collected things that had some intuitive appeal; perhaps they felt good in my hand; perhaps I was drawn to the way the light bounced off them; or maybe the mechanistic aspects of these natural or industrial parts, fragments, and artifacts produced a magnetic appeal for a young boy. As I grew older and stopped collecting, and started making things, I still found myself drawn to objects—especially ordinary everyday objects and things that addressed problems or helped people in different ways. I would and still do play a mental game of asking questions of the things I see. What could have been the thinking that led to the development of this object or that one? Why might someone have selected a particular material or form to deliver this idea? What might the purpose of a particular detail have been in a greater scheme? These questions open larger dialogues: How have we adapted to different environments and situations through built intervention? Why are decisions made that lead to the implementation of things from objects to architecture, systems to propositions? What happens when one material ends and another begins? Do we celebrate difference and transition or do we cultivate continuity? Thinking of my own childhood, I realize that as I contemplated objects and environments, I was beginning to think about the commonalities and differences in the structures that are the fabric of human evolution. Even then, I began to categorize objects into types of solutions.

Deep knowledge of history and the social sciences is a critical addition to the perspective of a designer, perhaps more so in today's complex world than ever before. I have come to think about this kind of process, drawing systematically from specific experiences, as analogous to the way an optometrist asks a patient to try on a series of lenses to find the best way of seeing. Like the optometrist, I use a series of lenses to solve design problems. It is my hope that explicating my design processes in this way can be helpful to others.

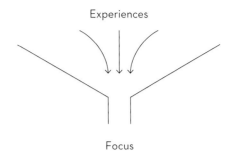

Experiences

Focus

Personal History

Both of my parents are the children of working-class immigrants. My father, who became a professor, was part of the first-generation in his family to attend university. Like many new immigrants, his parents sacrificed a lot and recognized the value of education for advancement. The emphasis on education continued with my own upbringing.

The summers of my formative years were spent traveling to the Middle East, participating with my father's students in archaeological excavations. As a result, I developed a work ethic and an eye for detail. I became curious about the world and its varied cultures, and open to experiencing its richness and diversity. Moreover, I learned the importance of documenting process and outcome. I learned that all artifacts of human endeavor, whether written, visual, architectural, sculptural, material or technological are key to garnering insights. As I worked alongside students and professionals, I observed how one assembles a record of divergent times and the histories of different peoples.

But it was the objects that had remained the same across the millennia that stayed with me the most. I don't mean object types. Although objects made for holding, storing, sitting, conveying information, and shelter indeed remain fundamentally similar across time and space, what I was most struck by were the details and dimensions of the objects themselves: the shapes of things that feel good in the hand or against the lips; the things that we can see up close and far away; the spaces we can fit through and those that we can't. We share these elements across cultures. They define us as human.

Enduring Objects

Solutions surround us. Sometimes it is challenging to see their beauty for their all-pervasive impact; sometimes it is challenging to see them for their quietness within the landscape of things. Solutions are not always contemporary, nor are they always what we think of as "design." And yet everything around us is design.

We must constantly be mindful of our history and our context in order to see objects clearly for their place in time. While materials and technologies change, human needs remain the same, as do the confines of our bodies and the scope of our physical abilities. So the past remains a continuum of opportunity for the present and for the future.

As designers, our job is to see what others do not— to make fluid and seamless connections between culture and commerce and to plant seeds that will grow. We are, in a way, the farmers of objects and systems. At our best, we plant and nurture seeds of the things that help us to live better, easier, and more enjoyably, and that fill our lives with beauty and purpose.

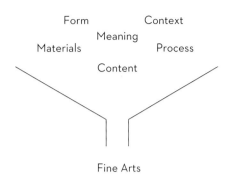

Form   Context
Meaning
Materials   Process
Content

Fine Arts

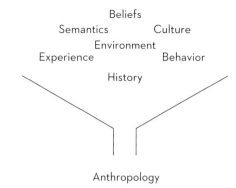

Beliefs
Semantics   Culture
Environment
Experience   Behavior
History

Anthropology

Distillation

While my father exposed me to the study of the built environment, my mother showed me the value of tactical and strategic organization. Like many women in her generation, my mother stayed at home with my brother and me. I often think that if she had been born in a different era, she might have been a CEO of a major corporation. She managed the ebb and flow of our day-to-day lives and, in some sense, my father's career as well. Because we did not have significant assets, my mother carefully weighed our options— both physical and conceptual—making choices and cultivating relationships that shaped our landscape of opportunities as we grew together. My mother is an exuberant optimist. As a result, we always felt rich in opportunity if not in material possessions. We had the things that were important to us and we understood how to prioritize our choices in order to pursue the goals we set for ourselves.

My mother has always had an ability to prioritize relationships among people, events, and things. It wasn't necessarily an effortless ability but it was often executed with elegance. This showed me that it is possible to make much from very little by distilling what is most essential and carefully aligning variables to maximize effect. Looking back, I believe these early lessons about priorities helped lay the groundwork for me to navigate complex challenges and find the essential ingredients for design solutions.

Distillation takes time. It begins with fostering strong relationships with others in order to clarify and refine the result. There is a funnel effect in how results are obtained. In the end, a well-executed result often reads as effortless when in fact it is the product of careful and tireless cultivation.

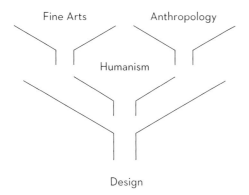

Fine Arts

Anthropology

Humanism

Design

Learning How to See

Without having any prior context for design as a career choice, I was not convinced that attending university immediately after high school was the right use of my time. Somehow my interests in understanding culture and making things did not seem to have a converging point of connection in the educational system. I felt pressure to choose between these things. Instead of going directly into a singular course of study, I decided to spend a year outside of the US in the hope of having experiences that would help me find a vocation that integrated my interests.

That year, however, did not provide answers; it raised more questions and wanderlust. While I signed up to take classes at Tel Aviv University, I also took every opportunity to travel, mostly through the western and southern border areas of Egypt, as well as to several small islands in the Mediterranean. I had little money, and took more than a few risks, visiting some remote and isolated villages—places that felt as if they were at the end of the world. I witnessed what life is like for those who live with few material resources in the harsh desert landscape. Back at Tel Aviv University, I took a course in animal reproduction. Because I had agile hand skills, I was designated as the class dissector. I explored the inner workings of animal bodies. I took another course on reef life of the Red Sea, in which we put on diving gear and learned by direct observation about the interdependence of ecosystems. I spent the year filling sketchbooks with drawings and written observations. I used my camera to record experiences. Taken together, these were impactful and life-changing experiences for me. Like many 18-year-olds, I was busy trying to triangulate my location and purpose in the world.

By the end of the year, I knew I was interested in learning more about human behavior and culture. I was also interested in giving form to materials and technology. I began studying at Cornell University, where I could work on two degrees concurrently. I chose anthropology and sculpture. What I did not know at the time I began university, was that these two paths actually intersect within the field of design.

In my third year of university, I won a scholarship to study for a semester in Rome, where I anticipated studying Renaissance master sculptors such as Michelangelo, Bernini, and Da Vinci. What I did not expect was to gather a deep knowledge of their work as architects, engineers, and graphic artists. They were all storytellers hired to work across various media to deliver important messages. This was of great value to me as I began to realize at this point that my interest in working across disciplines was mirrored in the focused approaches of these masters. It was here that I realized my path could take me into the field of design.

After finishing my undergraduate degrees, I chose to continue my education by filling in the gaps necessary to fully appreciate the occupation of design. In the furniture design master's degree program at the Rhode Island School of Design, I sought to refine my ideas and explore new modes of investigation. After graduation, I combined project work with teaching, as one practice began to inform the other, a template that defines my professional life today.

Lenses for Design

When you buy a pair of sneakers, you become keenly aware of the brand. Suddenly, everyone seems to own a pair with the same logo as yours. When I first considered lenses as a metaphor for refocusing the way people observe behavior and materials, in this same way the many actual lenses in my life began to appear in plain sight.

When I was very young, growing up in a small town in western New York, my parents took me to visit the Corning Museum of Glass nearby. While the stories and images of the history of the medium presented were impactful, and while I well remember being mesmerized watching the factory's glassblowers turn blobs of molten material into product before my eyes, one image endures: the world's largest piece of glass, a yellowish five-meter diameter, 20-ton circular object known as the 200-inch Disk. Made in a single casting in 1934, this item was designed to function as a mirror (an alternative method to gathering light from a lens), to gather light for the most powerful telescope ever created, the Hale Telescope, on Mount Palomar in California. This object was a giant step in technological innovation, made possible by pushing the limits of material, technology, and human capacity in an effort to see the universe differently by literally expanding sight in order to gain knowledge.

After many years living in other places, I am back in western New York, living just down the road from the 200-inch Disk. I now have many dear friends at Corning and have been fortunate to work with them, exploring the medium of glass through my own lens.

Shortly after moving to Rochester, I noticed a great example of a glass Coca-Cola bottle—an enduring object—among other items in an antique shop. I've always loved the shape, feel, and heft of the older Coke bottle designs from the 1940s, but I have never owned one. For a modest price, I purchased this one to add to my collection of well-designed, well-made things. Turning it over, I was surprised to find that it was manufactured locally in a bottling plant from years past. I paused to look through the very thick base and remembered the way people used to refer to prescription eyeglasses with very thick/heavy lenses as "Coke-bottle lenses." I remember standing in the store, viewing the world through a blue-green hue, the distorted images conveyed through the bottle's glass allowing me to see shapes of things around me as less defined, more ethereal, the edges of things blurring together. I was instantly reminded that sometimes seeing our surroundings less clearly is as important as seeing them with great focus.

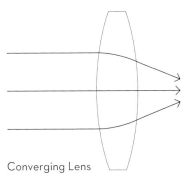

Converging Lens

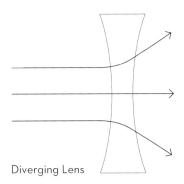

Diverging Lens

When I needed a magnifying glass to use for the imagery in this book, I scoured the Internet to find just the right one in a store halfway across the country. Examining it the day it arrived, I found that it was made here, in Rochester, at Bausch+Lomb, a company renowned across the world for making lenses. The serendipity of bringing this object back to its origins felt exactly right.

The giant mirror serves as an aid to a converging lens to help us to see farther, more clearly, and more precisely, revealing more than we knew previously. Looking through a Coke-bottle lens blurs what we knew previously, revealing a world of fluid beauty through its diverging quality. Both lenses are tools of variable perception. Between them lies a range of options for seeing. The magnifying glass is a human-scaled tool, a metaphor for adjusting one's focus.

Not a Finite Set

The lenses described in this book are not a finite set, nor are they categorically independent. I use them to categorize objects and approaches to design; but in truth, some objects fit in multiple categories and might be seen through various lenses.

The main section of this book describes and expands on the lenses that I have used to solve design problems. For each of these lenses—Sharp Focus, Soft Focus, Macro Focus, Micro Focus, Blurred Focus, and the Deconstructed Lens—I group objects of my design in order to offer insights into design process and outcomes.

Lenses
for
Design

Sharp Focus

Delivering a message that is direct and clear may be the most identifiable hallmark of what I think of as "good design" or "effective design communication." An object that appears in sharp focus emotes its function by way of its visual identity. Sharpness in this context, therefore, can mean the directness of the answer to the problem, clarity of the utility and form, or a combination of these factors. The projects that are described in the following section allow me to investigate ways of managing problem-solving and privileging clarity.

Cause and Effect

Tone Knob Lamp

The tactile, haptic response to objects we had become used to over millennia (e.g. consider the click of a light switch) has been replaced by encoded auditory effects, reactions communicated by color changes, and occasional vibration through touch-sensitive screens (e.g. the user interface of a smart phone). The future will see even more technical sophistication in this feedback loop and additional loss of tactile interaction in the traditional sense.

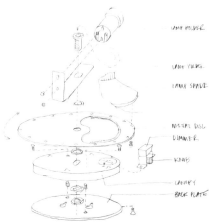

I designed the Tone Knob Lamp in 1996, when we were on the edge of the digital revolution. The lamp references the analog knobs still used on musical equipment and in industrial settings on things like vehicles and machines. When rotated, the oversized knob delivers more or less light. In this object, interface is directly connected to function, eliminating mediation. The haptic aspect of this product creates a satisfying emotional connection between user and device, delivering an enduring meaning, perhaps even more poignantly now than when it was conceived.

One of the challenges in making this a consumer product, which I designed for the Canadian manufacturer Umbra, was to distill a technically complex object into a relatively low-priced item. The simple act of adding a dimmable light source to an object of interface was new. Traditional incandescent bulbs produced copious amounts of heat. While cooler options such as dimmable compact fluorescent technologies for lighting were emergent, LEDs were only in development and not commercially accessible at that time.

So I began an investigation into heatflow. I sought simple mechanisms to deliver a reasonable amount of light for bedside applications. In the end, I specified stamped parts and an incandescent bulb to respond to the market for this product. Heat flow was managed by introducing a hole pattern along the top of the object and lofting the plastic lamp shell above the back plates. The Tone Knob Lamp also allowed for wall mounting, important from my perspective, to give a greater range of application.

I also wanted the power cord to mimic, as much as possible, an electric instrument cable, strengthening the association with musical instruments and stereo dials, both of which inspired the design. This sensitivity was critical to the product-naming strategy. In addition, the round section cord drapes elegantly, creating a clean, unkinked line in space, whether positioned to fall along a table or drift down a wall surface toward a power supply.

In the wall condition, the object takes on the identity of a control mechanism for the architecture of the room (to the extent that lighting is an element of the design of space). The idea was to close the gap between control and controller by allowing for a direct influence on the atmospheric effects of the room.

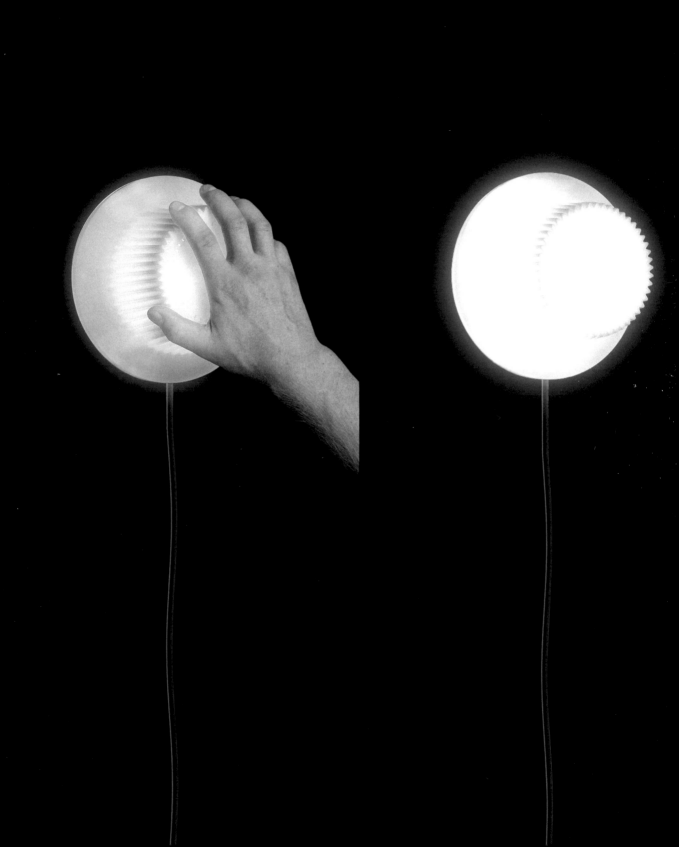

Creating Efficiencies

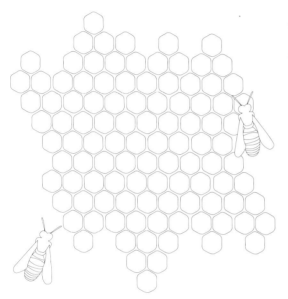

Cube Jigger

Good design is always a method for creating efficiencies; it makes things better by aligning elements of value and ultimately organizing our behaviors.

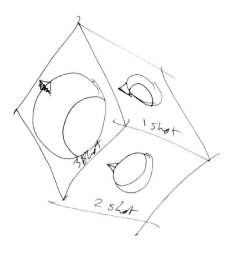

The design of the Aluminum Cube Jigger follows this search for object economy. It evolved from an experiment to compress the six most common liquid measurements used to mix alcoholic drinks into the smallest possible dispenser.

The traditional Japanese sake cube-shaped drinking vessel served as an inspiration for the overall shape of this project. The cube is an unlikely rectilinear shape for liquid containment. On first glance, box shapes are not conducive to holding liquids. Too many tight corners create hard-to-reach areas for cleaning and implausible emotional connections to the delicate qualities we associate with connecting our mouths to vessels. However, the Japanese sake cup served as an object lesson. That this unlikely shape could hold liquid and pour from its corners inspired me to proceed.

| 0.50 oz | 0.75 oz | 1.00 oz | 1.50 oz | 2.00 oz | 2.25 oz |

A careful look at the science of mixology revealed the bartender's need for speed in the process of measuring the amount of alcohol to be delivered in the recipes she delivers. Four measures are sufficient to complete most cocktails, but six allow for greater flexibility, particularly as mixing becomes more sophisticated and bartending becomes more like performance.

A jigger must be manipulable by a single hand (the other hand occupied by a bottle). A three-inch, six-sided cube fits into the average hand. Computer aided technology was extremely useful in determining relative volumes of each side of the cube by pushing and pulling the forms until the relative voids eluded intersection successfully.

Exploring Parameters

Flip Clip Report Cover

Product design often requires understanding of a multitude of different fields, including graphic design and architecture, business and the law, material science and engineering and psychology and anthropology. A good designer needs to take the time to understand the perspectives of people in these various contributory fields. Ideally, a designer can bring people together and facilitate communication in order to move ideas forward in meaningful and synergistic ways.

The exploration of definable parameters encompasses most of the research done in the pursuit of design solutions. Like describing points on a map before triangulating a position, establishing these parameters allows for the accurate location of opportunities for refinement that lead to elegant points of intersection.

This approach can lend clarity to the most befuddling of situations. One of my favorite examples of this pulling together of points into the form of a product is the Flip n' Clip report cover, created for Paris Business Products. At the time this item was introduced, most report covers were made to beautify documents by adding visual appeal and, therefore, perceived value and authority. But form and color alone, or the elevation of perceived value, are not enough to make an object meaningful, let alone functionally successful.

Exploring a different parameter—or lens—used to solve a design problem requires honest scrutiny. Standard plastic report covers assume that a report should look and act like a book, and use a binding along the side. While a book spine works for a book, a report is generally meant to be shared for commentary, e.g. by a teacher. Therefore, it should be able to lie flat when its pages are turned. It should be similarly easy for the user to turn pages without risking the document falling apart.

Using a different principal parameter (i.e. facilitating the process of reading and marking up a document), helped me define further points of reference. A stapled report, typically bound in the upper left corner for ease of folding, represents an ideal vehicle for its function. However, it is not protected by a cover. A manila folder does not require assembly, but also does not hold the documents securely. Given these well-tested points on the map, the challenge was finding their intersection.

Emerging from this intersection, the Flip n' Clip brings together the functional efficacy of a protective cover and the corner-binding capabilities of the staple, with the additional innovation of allowing users to customize their reports to either landscape or portrait format simply by flipping the report cover over.

One Way

Cheese Tool and Wooden Spoons

It is complex enough to consider creating a tool for a particular focused utility, but adding true multi-function requires the designer to manage various complexities while maintaining a sharp focus on the essence of the object.

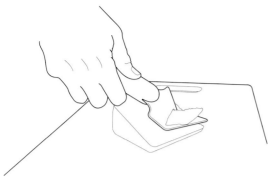
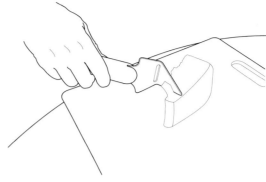

The Swiss Army Knife, a multi-function object that also has dual application—military and civilian—expresses simplicity in both function and design. The Swiss Army Knife succeeds as an elegant singular design even thought it packs enormous variety into a discrete package. In this case, the practicality of combining related functionalities in one easily accessable and compact unit is the essence of the object. The individual quality of each tool in the Swiss Army Knife maybe sacrificed, but this becomes less important if the essence of the object is preserved.

This same sacrifice is made by each of us when we multitask. Objects like the smart phone exploit our need to manage multiple things at once, but also enable it by making technology easier to manipulate, thereby reducing the sacrifice. The wonder of it—can you believe what you can do?—has conditioned designers to pursue multi-use solutions in product design.

It can be tempting as a designer to layer function upon function, as opposed to focusing on a singular action. The danger is that we pair too many dissimilar functions into a single object without considering the object's essence.

The consideration of singularity vs. multifunction guided my investigation of a cheese tool for Kikkerland. A complex language of devices governs worldwide culinary rituals associated with cheese. I was interested in creating a device that would function efficiently for the US market. I also wanted to combine common actions associated with serving cheese. The scope of ambition led to a design that paired two associated actions within a single device: cutting and slicing. In this case, the attention paid to these two actions without losing sight of the object's essense makes the final object intuitive.

In a related project, also for Kikkerland and again for the kitchen, the object of the wooden spoon tests the notion of multifunction.

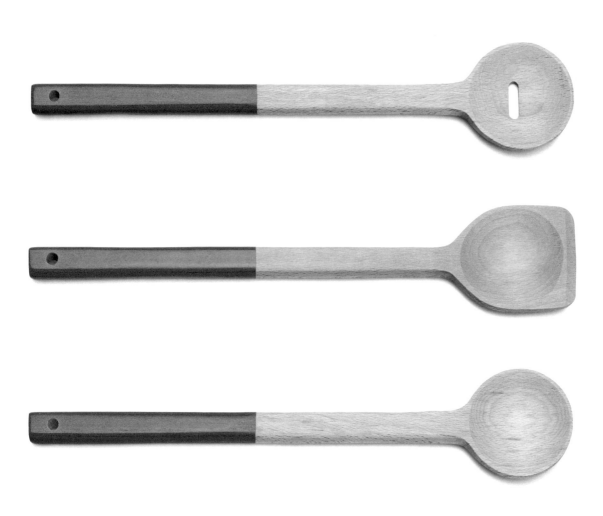

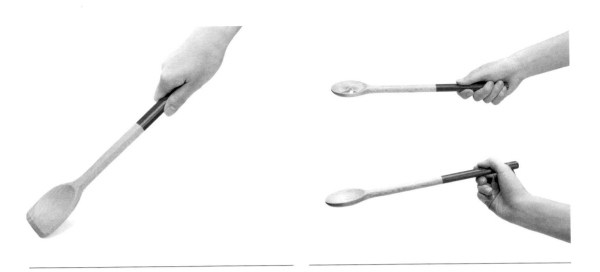

In the gadget-dominated kitchen products landscape, wooden spoons remain traditional and indispensable. The function of a wooden spoon can be distinct or universal, largely dependent on the details that are pushed in the design language. When developing this project, I sought to find the most essential functionalities in order to minimize the number of tools in the set: stirring, scraping, spooning, and a variety of lifting actions all appeared to be the most desirable qualities. This is a process of layering points of reference in order to reveal common applications. In other words, sharpening focus.

I found that several of these actions could be shared by a single spoon without sacrificing utility. For example, in the case of the corner spoon, I combined the actions of scraping and stirring by including an angled scraper with a profile sculpted for precise stirring. This also allows the spoon to act as a scraper while still carrying the round language of the spoon family set. The two remaining completely round spoons can also be paired as salad tongs.

The almost-round handle possessed by each of these spoons provides an easy and firm but directional grip. The bold Kikkerland red on the delicate beechwood suggests a hint of personality but is actually employed for durability to prevent staining in long-term usage.

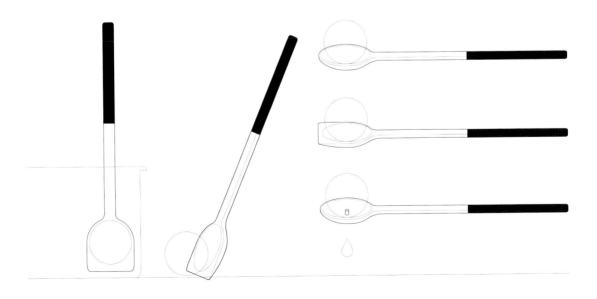

Soft Focus

The consideration of soft focus lies in the attention to emotional responses to objects. A function might be paired with a poetic connection to the object to evoke a reaction or engagement or deliver a message that pushes beyond the object's pragmatic function into the territory of meaning. The object then delivers a message beyond its practical use. Some of my projects privilege the element of soft focus in order to create a point of entry for target users.

Simple Pleasures

Corkscrew and Bottle Stopper

The answer to some problems should only be sharp enough that the conclusion feels intuitive, just as we generally agree that something sweet tastes good. A simple pleasure, such as enjoying a piece of fresh fruit, can produce a kind of universal understanding and corresponding effect.

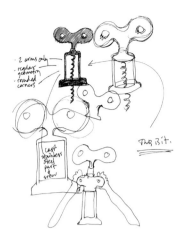

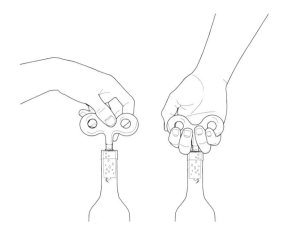

Wine, as a product to be enjoyed, can also fall into this category. While new materials and technologies have driven innovation in the industry, we could say that the fundamental act of consuming wine has not changed much over the millennia, nor has the process of opening a corked bottle. Thus, when I approached the subject of a wine bottle opener and stopper, I had no intention of attempting to change this overall behavior.

In my opinion, products on the market that attempt to expediate the activity of opening a wine bottle miss the basic point that enjoying wine should be a deliberate process to be savored. Pleasure is the soft focus I applied when I looked at the assignment to design a wine stopper and bottle opener for Kikkerland. In fact, it was useful to recognize through this lens that a bottle of wine perhaps is better uncorked slowly than quickly, a soft-focus technique.

The secondary focus was on pure functionality: the oversized handle is ergonomic, allowing for a comfortable grip and the ability to lever and remove the item with relative ease. While this is an imperative aspect of the functionality of the project, a visual cue is meant to trigger the memory of a children's toy wind-up key, reinforcing the idea of simple pleasure. When attached to the top of the bottle, the identity of the bottle is transformed into a playful object, turning the act of uncorking the bottle from a mundane task into a joyful event. Like a wind-up toy, turning the corkscrew is an act of anticipation.

Sometimes design is an act of measured appropriateness. Sometimes resisting the impulse to make things work "better" is valuable. Always, design should be about making enduring decisions.

Knockoff Lamp

Some objects in the world are so embedded in the cultural vernacular that they suggest certain behaviors, without thought. A light switch begs to be flipped on or off. The bowling pin is standing; therefore, the bowling pin should be knocked down. The pin tells us one story when it is standing and one story when it is lying down. These stories become a lens for seeing the object, as does the tactile and playful nature of bowling. The Knockoff Lamp I designed originally for Bozart, and later for Kikkerland, was an experiment in using the idea of playfulness to shortcut and make more immediate a legacy object—the lamp that is controlled by a mediating agent, the switch. What if we cut out the liaison?

A traditional on-off lamp contains the same binary experience as the bowling pin. In its standing state, a bowling pin is waiting to be knocked over. When it is knocked over, it waits to be stood back up. Taking its cue from this iconic shape, when the Knockoff lamp is on its side, the light is off. When the pin stands up tall, it glows. The activity becomes the switch.

Shifting the identity of an object entirely to create a condition where an object looks in some way "unfinished" is an important discovery here. In the same way that one would gravitate toward adjusting a plant that has fallen over, the user feels the need to interact with the object.

Bowling is an addictive game—once you recognize your power to clear the pins, you want to do it again and again. The lamp, not unlike the bottle opener, draws its utility from pleasurable memory and capitalizes on the our desire to recapture that pleasure.

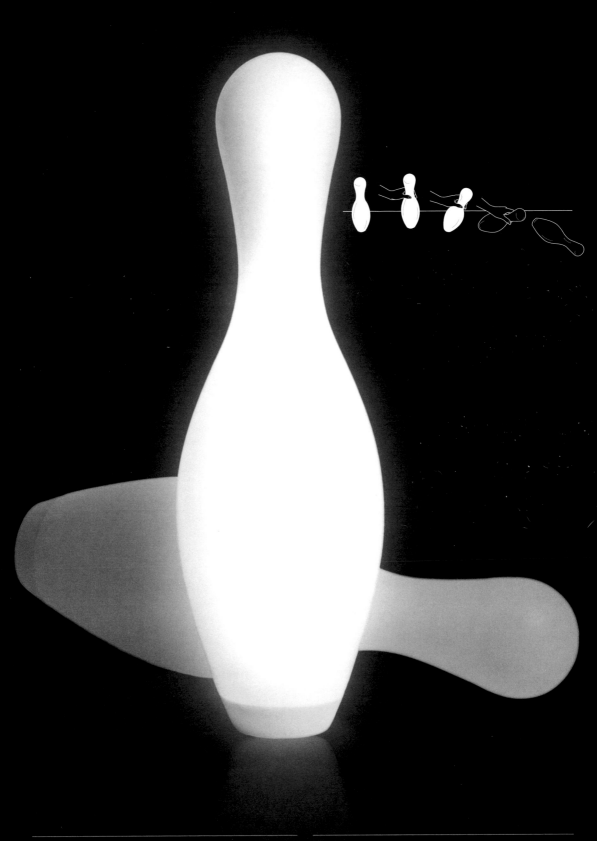

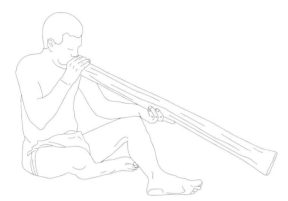

Moneypig Bank

How can designers and end users agree on a form's ability to communicate an idea? Is it possible for designer and user alike to dream the same dream? If so, then it is likely because the designer somehow has tapped into the collective unconscious. This is how I came to form the parameters of the Moneypig Bank, designed for Bozart.

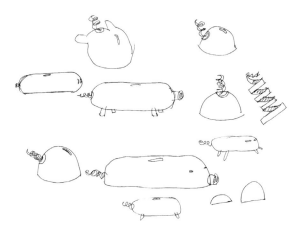

To find resonance with the notion of a collective unconscious, it's helpful to consider the example of the dream world of Australian Aborigines. Many indigenous Australians refer to the creation of the world as "The Dreaming." Here are stories about creation of places, people, animals, plants, laws, land, and customs. Reinforcing this as shared consciousness is "the walkabout," a rite of passage. Adolescent boys live in the wilderness for a period as long as six months. In this practice, they trace the paths, or "songlines," that their ancestors once took, and imitate, in a fashion, their heroic deeds.

The walkabout is part of a complex network of knowledge, faith, and practices that derive from stories of creation. It pervades and informs all spiritual and physical aspects of an indigenous Australian's life. Traditional Aboriginal art almost always has a mythological undertone relating to the Dreamtime of Australian Aborigines.

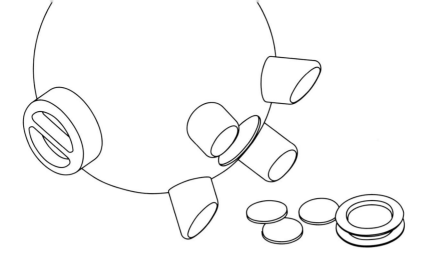

Western cultures have their own dreamtimes. In the US, Hollywood's cinematic vision and the imagery of Madison Avenue are powerful generators of the collective unconscious, producing common archetypes. The dreamscape is, in fact, filled with objects. It is here that I drew on the archetypal symbol of the piggy bank for the Moneypig Bank.

The form of this coin holder probes the collective unconscious vision of the friendly cartoon pig. Taking advantage of this form-language, the pig's bloated orb shape allows the coins to naturally slide toward and spill out of its underbelly when the plug is removed, no shaking necessary.

Serious Play

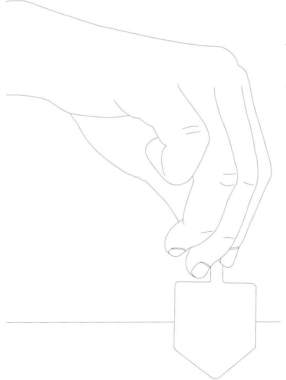

Magnito and Graphic Sox

The word play has many connotations, all associated with action and enjoyment. A playful object evokes joy or humor or promises to engage the imagination in some way. When used as a design lens, play can be employed as a mechanism for provocation, inciting interaction or eliciting response. I think of play, in this form, as being different than wit. Punning as a lens won't necessarily produce enduring objects. Play, on the other hand, requires a deeper level of engagement.

The alluring and playful effect produced by a spinning top inspired the design of the Magnito salt and pepper shaker for Kikkerland. This project began as an investigation into ways to appropriate the thrill of child's play for what some might consider to be monotonous: the ritual of the family meal. The hope was to inject a measure of irreverence into a formal context. The lens of play is a like a window on a distant memory and that lens in turn suggests the language of the object.

Made up of two halves, this object clicks together and pulls apart to reveal separate salt and pepper shakers. As a combined form at rest on the table, the unit behaves like a gently rotating top. When clicked apart, two halves emerge, one labeled by an "S" and the other by a "P," delineating their contents. Each has holes with different orbits, which keep the salt and pepper isolated in their containers when joined.

The Magnito salt and pepper shaker is a good example of the limits of multi-functionality. While the object performs well for storage and use, keeping the two halves together, it isn't also, and shouldn't be, a spinning top. Certain lenses don't converge.

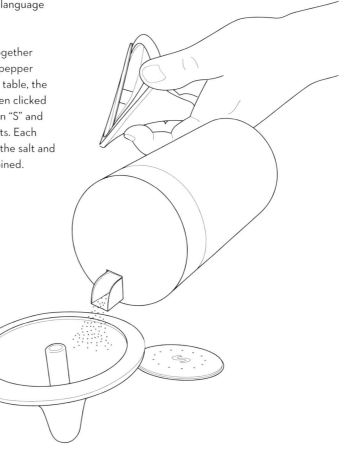

Although a salt and pepper shaker perhaps shouldn't also be a toy, can a sock be a message board? Only if the message redounds to the meaning of a sock itself. Extraneous messages, or gestures, become only trash. Again, lenses must align, as they did in the creation of Graphic Socks for SoxBox, which reflects an opportunity to bring levity to banality. Like a tattoo, the strategic ornamentation and signage developed for these gift socks can communicate like a shared secret, perhaps discovered from across a subway car.

Here a sock becomes a message board for personal statement, capable of commenting on the human condition, referencing history, or simply riffing on the act of walking.

Applied Metaphysics

Chiaroscuro Clocks

Metaphysics attempts to clarify the fundamental notions by which people understand the world. By applying a metaphysical lens to the design of objects, we place objects in a context where their behavior is influenced by external factors that drive outcomes fundamental to their cause.

In a designed object, the metaphysical factors should align with other factors, such as utility and functionality; this is a way of finding simple. While time is an artificial construct, measuring it generally is a tactical expression of our best attempts at visual communication. In the case of the Chiaroscuro Clock I designed for Loll Designs, daylight—the external object, a measure of time—illuminates the keeping of time itself.

Chiaroscuro is Italian for the combined effect of light and dark. It is also a technical term used by artists and art historians to describe the use of contrasts of light to achieve a sense of volume in modeling three-dimensional forms. Light defines the character of these clocks by the changing shadow effects produced by the engraved number forms and the use of chiaroscuro in the design itself creates clarity of vision. And while the clocks represent clarity in communication, they also offer a subtle shifting of personality as the changing natural and ambient light manipulate the expressions of the clock face.

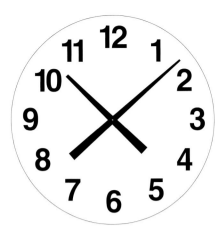

The Chiaroscuro Clock seeks harmony in a digital age suffused with timekeepers that distract and absorb your conscious attention. Waking in the morning to glance at a substantial feature on the wall, catching the early light of the sun, or unconsciously marking the minutes left until breakfast, must give way to the next stage of the day. These are all the tasks of something larger than our smartphones. And perhaps more appropriate.

Once we reach to check our devices for the time, we are likely to fall further into the digital landscape, perhaps missing the beauty of the precious moments at the breakfast table while savoring both food and company.

Macro Focus

In photographic terms, the macro lens allows for extreme close-up views. However, macro can also mean "to take the long view" or to view things as if they were seen from above, as one would look at a city from the window of an ascending airplane. In many of my projects, designed objects depend heavily upon the landscape in which they exist. In some cases, they simply could not perform without this context.

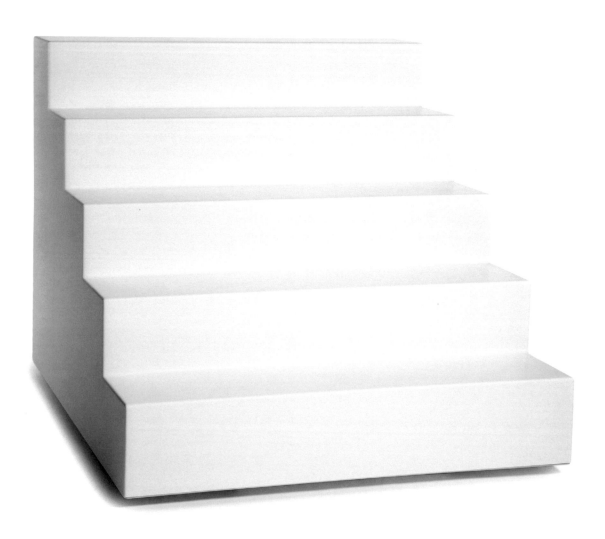

Considering the Void

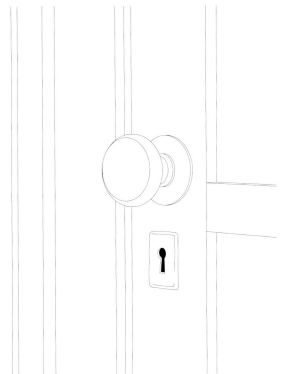

Stoop Bench and Bookend Picture Frame

In 2009, DuPont's Corian division asked me to create a public bench in Philadelphia as part of the annual design fair, Design Philadelphia. Immediately, I thought of the form and place of the front stoop, ubiquitous in that city. The stoop bench emerged when I considered the void left by urban development that ignores the need for community gathering spaces in certain places in the city.

Besides its selection for its obvious durability and proximity for harvesting, the gleaming white marble of many stoops in Philadelphia creates an alluring quality that beckons us to do more than walk on them. "Sit, please," they seem to say. The bright whiteness of the material softens its identity in an urban context and the cool feel of the stone engages its occupants and draws us to connect with the material while we sit, caressing its surfaces and edges.

Though both stoop and bench are liminal places where people come and go, the stoop has a magnetic quality that draws people together for socializing. Residents come outside to enjoy warm weather and discuss neighborhood events or to watch a passing parade or street fair, and parents use them to keep an eye on children playing on sidewalks and in alleys.

With the stoop as a starting piont, how might a designer rethink the bench? Moving the essence of the stoop from the rowhouse grid into a different urban context seemed like a meaningful challenge. The experience of the stoop could be translated to a park or perhaps into a district without stoops, where businesses thrive and, although there is ample opportunity for social behavior, there might be little room to sit.

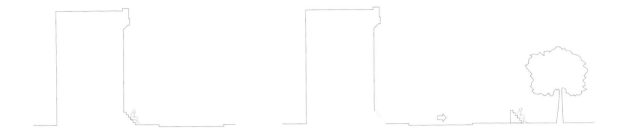

Structure discourages group dialogue

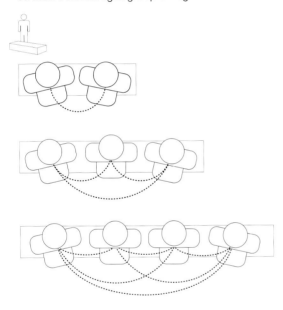

Structure facilitates group dialogue

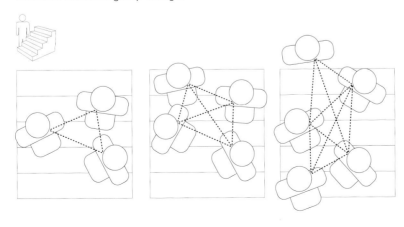

Part of the challenge in distilling a form for this "bench" was in attempting to capture the scale and proportions of an idealized stoop, while thinking of it as a kind of a product. Most urban benches allow for people to sit next to one another—three or four across. The stoop creates opportunities for small groups. Yet because of its height, people also can stand and talk with those who are perched on the higher tiers. Users can spread out to accommodate a number of different positions suited for different sorts of activities. Designing a temporary stoop for the public realm creates a new setting for private social interactions that could bridge the gap between the two realms.

Carefully considering the void in one environment forces one to look to existing solutions in parallel contexts, creating new opportunities.

Similarly for Kikkerland, I was considering the void created by bookends at the end of a shelf. I began to imagine a bookend that had the functionality of a picture frame (so as not to waste space or lose a visual opportunity). Like the original metal office bookends from which they take their general form, these would be created with an economy of materials and manufacturing in mind. Aside from the glass, no additional parts were added to the Bookend Picture Frames, keeping production waste to a minimum.

Like the stoop bench, the picture frame also transforms a standard typology, lending a visual dimension and animating a banal architectural space.

Mutualism

Flyswatter and Hanging Door Stopper

Objects do not exist in isolation; their dependencies are multifaceted and complex. I use the term mutualism to describe the lens through which to view the relationships between objects and the environments in which they are designed to function. There are many ways to consider such co-dependencies; most are probably so commonplace that we fail to consider them: the rug that needs the floor, the picture frame that needs the wall, the pillow that needs the bed. On close inspection, we discover that these sorts of relationships are practically inexhaustible if considered as a matrix for uncovering opportunity. My particular interest has been in the investigation of existing conditions. I want to uncover opportunities for objects to realize their potential for greater performance.

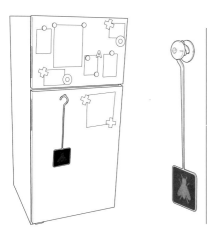

Take the case of the common flyswatter, an object category that, because of its unhygienic quality, is typically kept out of sight. The predisposition to hide such a tool creates the primary problem for its lack of efficacy: if one has to search for a tool for this kind of job, one already might have missed the opportunity to perform the job. So the question becomes: How can the object be transformed to overcome this obstacle? Seeing the solution requires another macro lens, this one to help us see object relationships.

The design of my Flyswatter for Kikkerland exploits the relationship between a doorknob/handle and a hook. The simple flyswatter appears to belong with the door handle because of the scale of the hook. To further extend the relationship to its surroundings, I embedded a two-sided magnet in the hook in order to create an affinity for metal surfaces.

Usual brightly colored flyswatters sold in the hardware store are made to attract the buyer's eye. But only a dark brown or black will hide bug residue. I chose a simple black, which also adds graphic readability to the hole pattern that illuminates the target.

Other aspects of the design process might be taken for granted: the weighting of the object, tapering and pliability, the determination of surface area of the head. The object must work, and it must perform well, besides any other modifications to the object classification that might enhance its utility.

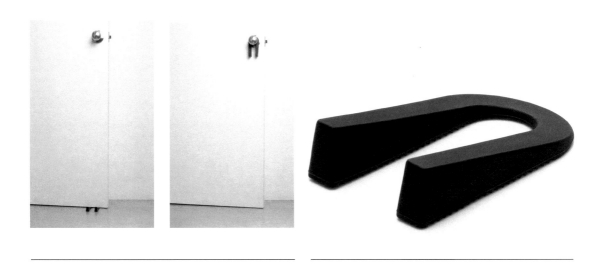

The hole pattern of a typical flyswatter is nondescript. Perhaps it helps conceal a mess. But it is also a missed opportunity. What else might overcome the instinct to hide away this object? Pictographic reference. This Flyswatter tells the user (and perhaps the visitor to her house) what the tool is for.

Another example of this mutualism is the case of the Hanging Door Stopper for Areaware. The principal problem with most doorstoppers is that they lack a home when not in use. Shuttling this object to one side creates a tripping hazard and is unsightly. I have never had a particular problem with the utilitarian form and function of the existing stopper archetype. Instead of designing an ornamental solution to this problem, I decided to see the problem through the lens of object relationships, this time again involving a doorknob/handle. Now the doorstopper spreads wider to accommodate its hanging position without sacrificing functionality.

Much as I gave the Flyswatter a graphic identity to associate the object with its use, the Hanging Door Stopper communicates its natural association with the door through its form language. It is made from extremely durable silicone, which has a high tearstrength and can be washed with soap and water. Most importantly, the shape leaves its intended user with a question whose answer is easily determined by its context. "Ah, it rests on the doorhandle when not in use," it seems to say.

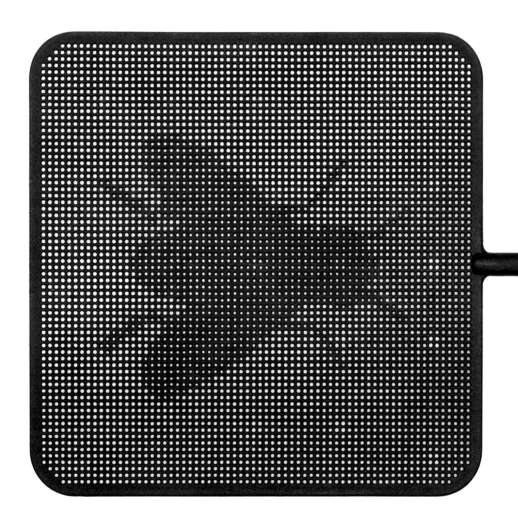

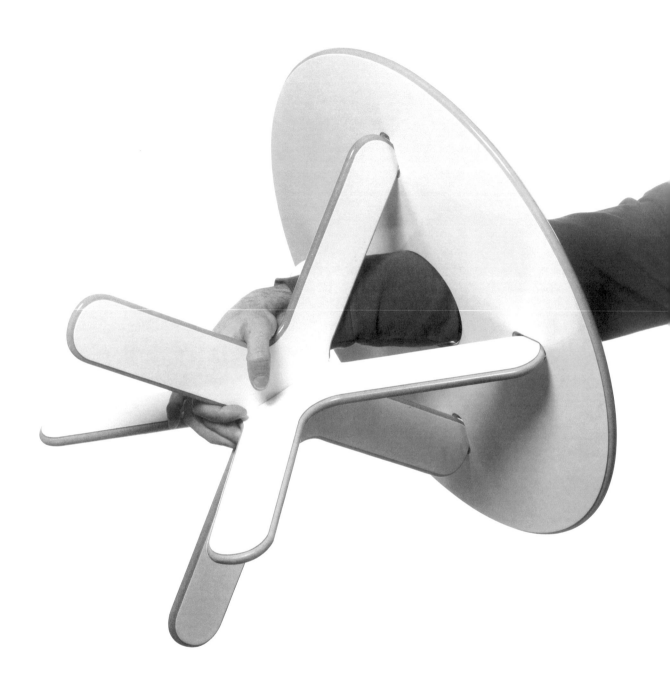

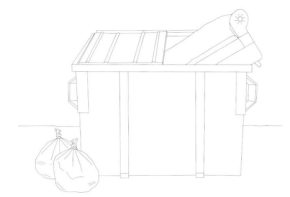

XOX and XX Furniture

As I begin to negotiate what we tend to collectively refer to as midlife, I have become more curious about the parallels I have noted in the lifespan of objects. Many products are designed to achieve peak performance early in their lifespan. As they endure the repetitive actions and movements associated with most products, many degrade and need to be disposed of and replaced. On the other hand, some objects appear to age more gracefully. Think of the century-old wooden bowl, still functional, perhaps even more desirable than when conceived, covered now with what some archaeologists refer to as "use-patina." The things in midlife lens are characterized by anticipating the stressors and environmental impacts associated with use.

With the XOX furniture line originally developed for Bozart, I began a series of research projects that investigated lifespan planning. At the time I was developing this furniture line, I noticed the preponderance of advertising for inexpensive furniture. Everywhere, it seemed, were items designed for planned obsolescence, limited lifespan, and a singular context.

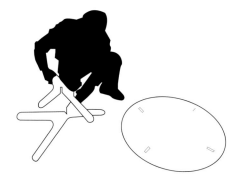

It occurred to me that if I could identify the areas of an object with the greatest risk for damage and atrophy, I could capitalize on this in order to create an opportunity for design development. For the purposes of this discussion, I will refer to these areas as functional detailing.

I designed the XOX Table foremost to be a mobile object. Having the ability to be transported easily both from the standpoint of the consumer and from the position of the manufacturer creates certain challenges. Considering a coffee table an "impulse purchase" on the part of the consumer was one of the primary inspirations for making it break down easily and pack flat. Realizing that most damaging activity occurs during assembly and during the packing/moving process, I looked for a synergistic relationship with a material.

The rather ubiquitous fiberboard, constructed primarily of waste material from the lumber industry, is economical and strong (it is made in sheets of varying thickness). Rarely has fiberboard been considered an aesthetic material, likely because of its generic brown color and perhaps its lack of grain or discernable structure. Its predecessor and counterpart, plywood, has, on the other hand, become an aesthetic material, probably because of the wood grain face, suggesting a more natural appeal.

It was this generic brown-colored material, in the end, that inspired the XOX Table's functional detailing that helps the product endure. Instead of covering the edges with lacquer paint or laminate edge-banding (adding extra cost and assembly concerns), I chose to allow this brown material to show through as a visual detail and in fact wrapped the areas of connection as well as edges where most typical damage would occur. The scuffing from use, assembly, and disassembly is hidden by the brown edges, allowing the design to continue to look new despite the temporal reality of middle age.

Like a person with a careful strategy for eating healthy and staying active, this object anticipates its potential for wear and tear by embracing it and celebrating its use-patina without appearing to age.

Both the XX Coat Rack and the XOX Coffee Table are extensions of the research begun for Bozart that culminated in the XOX Coffee Table for Casamania. Both items continue to explore creating efficiencies in design, manufacturing, and distribution. However, in the case of these two items, the strategy was to align more closely with the company's target audience—the luxury home market. Therefore, I looked for a more substantial finishing treatment / process to address the varied functions. For the coffee table, a smooth, hard surface was desirable and a lacquer finish was suitable to complete the object for easy, repeated cleaning. For the coat rack, however, I chose to employ a rubberized coating to create friction between objects. In this way, surface tension keeps gauzy scarves or wet towels from slipping or blowing off.

These objects were designed to be both classic and affordable (within their market segments) pieces of furniture. Relying on a simple manufacturing strategy, both products are constructed from several pieces of cut, sheet fiberboard. There is little tooling or assembly involved. They pack flat, making their journey from the factory to the end user a cost-effective one—and delivering longer life. The use of more robust painting techniques builds upon the logic of the first XOX Table—made to endure.

 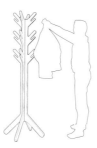

Macro Focus
Things in Mid-Life

Proximal Relationships

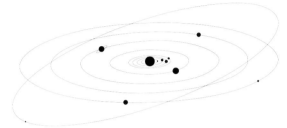

Bottle Opener

The landscape of objects that surrounds us demands synchronicity. Individuals cultivate their environments according to a logic. Known or subliminal, people make decisions based on a series of personal preferences that guide their aesthetic contructs. Eventually the objects and environments begin to have their own dialogues. The orbits of functionalities that connect these objects to their utility can be tracked and their intersections can on occasion lead to a powerful opportunity. This opportunity can be viewed through a kind of super-powered object relationship lens— I'll call it the proximal relationship.

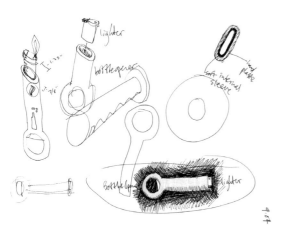

When I was asked by Kikkerland to develop a bottle opener, I was particularly interested in observing how this conventional object might exist within a stream of activities. Since it is most commonly used in the kitchen, I began my study there, where workflows overlap from food preparation to dining to socializing. While looking at the matrix of activities, I discovered no natural, or synchronistic, place to keep a lighter. Could it be paired with a proximal object? A standard lighter and my Bottle Opener are similar in size and associated in use (light a candle, open a bottle). Joined together, the probability that one or the other would be lost was decreased greatly. In fact, now that these two items depend upon each other and a common host (the magnetic surface of a refrigerator for example), they create a clearer potential for use.

This bottle opener and container considers the proximal relationship between drinking beverages with this type of closure cap and the use of a lighter in an environment where candles may be present. While its magnetic surface clings to the face of a refrigerator for easy access, the magnet also prevents the bottle cap from flying off while being removed.

Understanding the relative relationships between tools and rituals, flow of activity, and architecture can reveal opportunity. In this case, the co-dependencies between the tools aid one another in a more accessible outcome for the product.

Finding those synergies was the byproduct of a process of stacking lenses for design and mapping the overlapping orbits of activity in a given context. This environment-centered stragegy easily compliments a human-centered approach to design. Once the relationships are galvanized, the human factors can be folded easily into the development of the actual object.

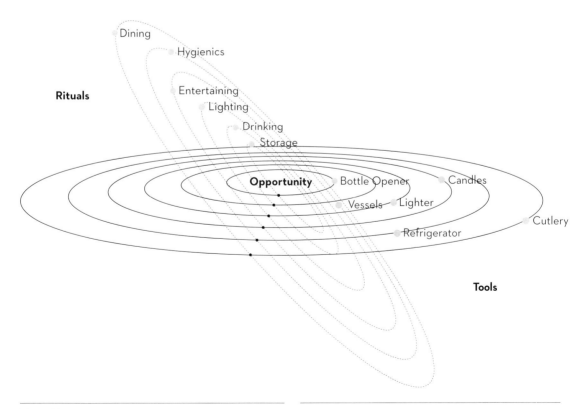

Micro Focus

Micro focus brings us to the level of the DNA of products. Where do ideas come from? A chair does not emerge from the designer's pen. A chair emerges from millennia of trial and error from countless individuals and groups attempting to solve similar problems in different contexts with different material, technological, and cultural constraints.

Anachronistic Adaptation

Twopart Chair

I am not a Luddite. Actually, when it comes to materials and technological advancement, I am something of a cautious optimist. As such, I embrace emergent technology because of its potential benefit to humans and to the planet.

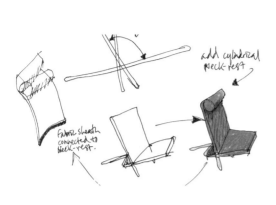

However, the technology that allows us to produce almost anything a human can need and much that one really doesn't need—at times collides with the physical limitations of our bodies, our lives, and our planet.

Being conscious of this fact, in an era when technology empowers us to give form to many of our wildest fantasies, necessitates a return to enduring principles and, therefore, the refinement of similar themes or archetypes. In other words: just because we can do something does not mean we should do it. Perhaps, then, ethics is an overall filter for design, as we weigh utility and expression. The ethical filter might promote usefulness in overall form, materiality, and function.

I use the term anachronistic adaptation to refer to a lens that captures the idea of re-invention or returning to a solution from the past. This lens often emerges in the process of historical research. One occasionally finds an elegant but forgotten solution designed to solve an enduring need.

For example, consider an object for sitting, a function which has remained fairly consistent for centuries. The Twopart Chair grew out of research into an ancient archetype. The ingenious design is thought to have originally evolved in sub-Saharan Africa. In that version, two slabs of wood depend upon each other structurally at the simple intersection of a square peg and a square hole. My version adapts the design for contemporary materials and uses. Unlike the standard high-end lounge chair, the Twopart Chair, with its sling seat, is designed to disassemble. It takes up a minimal amount of space, reduces the cost of shipping, and allows the end user to carry it out of a shop without much effort.

benza new york

Graphic Clocks

As an educator and as the father of two children, I have long been curious about the role a product can take in educating its consumers, regardless of the demographic or constituency. When we think of an analog clock, for example, the numbers can be used to teach children only after they can identify numerals. When I was asked by Benza to create some products using the clock face "as a canvas" for graphic treatment, I considered this question. I imagined that these clocks would fit into the context of a child's room, where play would engage the child in learning numbers and the concept of time.

I then wondered if it would be possible to enter into a visual dialogue with a young child around the topic of telling time while appealing to a more general audience with a graphic suggestion that would capture interest. Several of the designs I submitted were accepted for production.

The Time Flies clock encourages children and adults to count. Though it may appear that the graphic portrays a random collection of houseflies, here they are employed in the act of keeping time. The title, Time Flies, plays on the ephemeral nature of time itself, a notion reinforced by the sense that the insects have paused momentarily. Here, a sense of humor is carefully chosen to help distill the concept and enhance meaning through the lens of teaching tools.

The Doing Time clock also plays on humor by alluding to the prisoner scrawling out the passing days in a prison cell. Doing Time suggests the act of doing—counting—by making the marks that add up to the numbers they represent.

While not as obvious as a standard clock with Roman numerals, the mental work involved in discerning the information provided in these clocks is precisely the point. Observation, if couched in playfulness, can deliver emotionally satisfying tools for teaching.

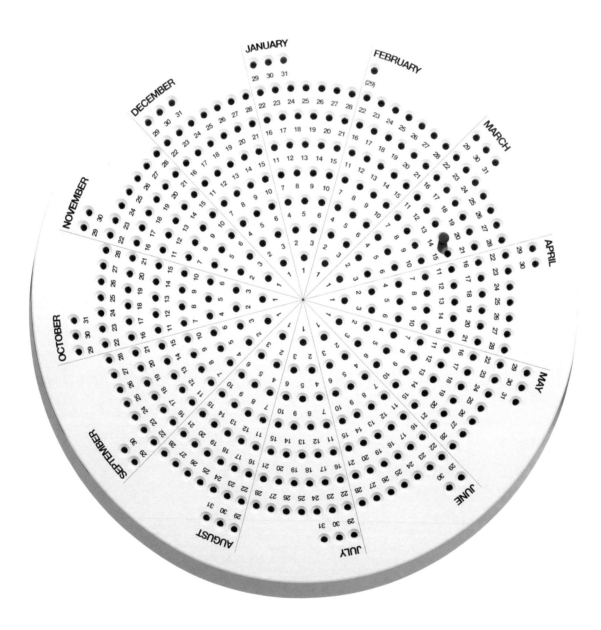

Analog Life

Perpetual Calendar

Analog rituals that previously managed our lives such as watches, clocks, datebooks, have mostly dissolved into the interface of digital devices. Because of the intangible nature of digital interfaces, management, meant to be simplified, often feels overly complex. The analog life lens offers a return to more concrete solutions.

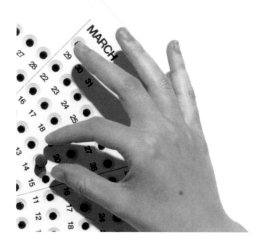

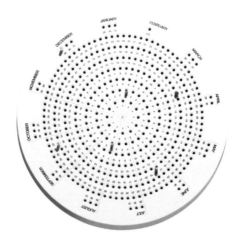

Digital calendar apps imagine that, for example, four members of a family could each share a calendar, with events and alerts. But the role of third parties—bosses, friends, associates—in scheduling complicates matters dramatically. Our ability to personalize preferences has reached such a level of complexity that even the simple act of telling time or location can cause serious injury or even death (I'm alluding to people's propensity to multi-task while driving). Would it be safe to say that we have created so many options so quickly that our ability to collectively exercise judgment has been impaired?

Many rely so heavily on digital assistants that things as simple as turning on a light switch or putting a key into a lock have become fetishized to the point of immense complexity (for example, from a hotel room in Milan one can control the lights in one's New York house). All these new realities rely upon a fragile infrastructure that might be easily corrupted and require attention that goes far beyond the average consumer's skill set. The critical lens we designers need to use, then, is one that helps discern appropriateness to context.

This Perpetual Calendar does not attempt to save the world, or to solve all of the problems I describe above. What it does is clearly present our place in time, looking across the scope of the year. Like a pin on a map, it gives the user a glimpse of context and triangulates our position within a larger continuum.

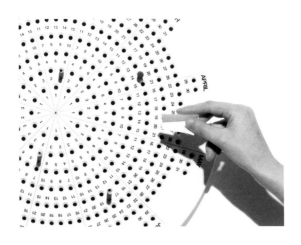

Many perpetual calendars are based on typographical cues, numbers that can be shifted. Many more are positioned in various linear formats. This product suggests the cyclical nature of time. Like a traditional clock whose hands turn around in continual movement, the peg works its way down and around the shape of this item without beginning or end. Like a traditional analog clock, the 12th month of December is oriented on the top of the wall-mounted object, further creating an affinity for a device we've grown accustomed to, with similar intervals.

Furthermore, the peg-in-holes design allows for a secondary function. Rolling up small notes to insert into holes creates an alternative language of information. One might indicate important dates, such as birthdays, anniversaries, and holidays, forcing herself to unscroll the information as she moves the peg ever closer to the indicated dates.

This analog perpetual calendar brings the ritual of seeing oneself in a larger order of magnitude than a standard clock into view. At the same time, it engages users to participate in a visceral way with positioning themselves in the scope of the year.

Ritual Objects

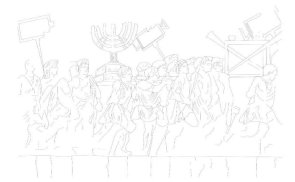

Menorah

Growing up participating in archaeological excavations, taught me to look carefully at both ceremonial and utilitarian objects. I've noticed differences and similarities and points where the categories become blurry. I've unearthed them, reconstructed them, and deconstructed them as well as evaluated and observed them in collections and in their functional locations. Often, images of these artifacts appear as ornamentation on monumental architectural structures, funerary sarcophagi, and even on products themselves, extending the life of objects into visual narrative, further revealing their original intended uses.

Because of the value humans place on ritual objects, they occupy special places in the context of our lives. Sometimes they live with us in our homes but are utilized only a few times in a calendar year; or they are relative to a particular event in a life cycle. Sometimes, ritual objects are site specific or located permanently in special buildings dedicated to a particular cause associated with spirituality. While not all ritual objects are associated with religion, all have highly specialized uses and are meant to emote certain values along with delivering the functionality tied to their purpose. Imagining the life narrative of a ritual object is a lens for design.

In 2000, through the ritual object lens, I began investigating the menorah, as I often do, by looking at historical examples of the typology. The illustration on the first page of this section represents the frieze on the Arch of Titus in Rome. This arch was constructed circa 82 AD by the Roman Emperor Domitian shortly after the death of his older brother Titus, to commemorate Titus' victories, including the sacking of Jerusalem in 70 AD. On the south panel, the image of the siege includes a depiction of the spoils taken from the Temple there. The Golden Candelabra, or Menorah, is featured prominently in the frieze. Because this is the only image of the actual Menorah attributed to the story of Hanukkah, it was a natural starting point for my design process. Could a modern menorah maintain a strong connection to this historical icon?

Like the re-crafting of ancient typography, my challenge began with developing a readable symbol. After working out the shape as a two-dimensional mark, I adjusted it and its proportions to follow regularized geometry. Once I found the mark to be scalable and highly identifiable as a menorah shape and symbol, I moved along to three-dimensional design and material challenges.

Because I hoped that the form could be the compelling element of this design, I focused on an industrial material rather than a precious one. The Menorah is made of solid cast iron and has the heft expected of such a material, but also a humility rare in ritual objects that more typically are made from expensive material meant to feel valuable. The iron's weight gives the Menorah a sense of solidity and self-worth, like a trusted tool found on a family farm. The singularity of the iron material suggests this object could age and continue to look even more beautiful as it acquires a patina from continual use.

Finally, after observing friends and family place their menorahs on plates to catch dripping wax, I incorporated a plate into the design that also provides a safe resting place for a used match.

Micro Focus
Ritual Objects

Blurred Focus

Not all projects are meant for general consumption. Nor are all designs complete thoughts, connecting stakeholders to end users. I've found great relevance in experimentation over the years. New technology, materials or approaches can inspire works of conceptual rigor that may not be commercially viable. Answering competitions of social or intellectual value can inspire change or move a larger dialogue forward. I refer to this section as blurred focus, acknowledging the propositional relevance of the output to follow as experimental.

Visual Sampling

Unbook Bank

While the idea of sampling (especially in music) is nothing new, it certainly has taken on new meaning in the context of digital culture. The fluidity with which we are able to access and generate content has reached a level of epic transparency, given the access the global community has to mobile phones capable of capturing and sending images, sounds and video.

During the course of my professional career, I have witnessed and participated in the advent of a complete shift in the flow of information. This new digital landscape quickens the pace and scale of communication while enabling an almost unfiltered deconstruction of text, history, culture, and imagery. In this context, vetting content is now becoming more challenging than acquiring or generating it. As technology disrupts traditional systems, forms, and objects, how do we as designers choose what to value? Using the sampling lens allows the designer to combine iconic items in order to create new contingencies and add new value.

I used the sampling lens to design the Unbook Coinbank/Bookend for Casamania. While the idea of a coin bank has proven its relevance over time, perhaps it was more desired when coins were paramount to paper money. As we stand poised to dispense with hard currency almost entirely, the landscape of dependencies has shifted around this object. Ironically, the value of the raw metal in some cases outweighs the value of the currency itself.

These parameters are recognizable in another legacy object, the book, whose economics have been destroyed by technology. I sought to align books and coins with the Unbook Coinbank/Bookend, a bookend that derives its weight from the coins deposited inside. Sampling the form was a matter of considering the factors that make up our idealized notion of the look and feel of a book. The affinity created by allowing coins to live together with books seemed natural.

Adaptive Reuse

CD Lamp

As global society comes closer to the acceptance that our planet is in serious peril from a lack of careful attention, many strategies for reconciling man's desires and their impact upon the planet are beginning to emerge. Adaptive reuse is a lens which allows us to identify opportunities for transitional or even obsolete materials before they are simply thrown away. The CD Lamp was an experiment in applying the adaptive reuse lens.

I was born during the end of the era of vinyl records. I witnessed the repurposing of the turntable as a musical instrument and vinyl records heated and twisted into jewelry. When the CD arrived, it represented a major step in technological evolution while still containing vestigial references (like the circular shape) to its predecessor. I was immediately interested in the packaging. Because of the mysterious nature of digital encoding (vinyl was more intuitive due to its visible grooves and bumps employed to transmit sound), consumers were puzzled about how to interact with CDs. Packaging and sleeves of all kinds were developed to suggest a mode of operation. As the CD itself has mostly disappeared, at least from the American market, the containment and packaging system known as the Jewel Case probably made the most visible imprint on the industry.

These plastic cases came in all colors and configurations, but the most common paired a clear front to accommodate the printed graphic insert, which told the story of the contents, with an opaque back, presumably to hide the back of the CD and to clearly indicate the front for shelving purposes. With the steady dematerialization of CD-based data storage, most of these jewel cases have been sent to the landfill. With ecology in mind, this project investigates repurposing the industrial artifact beyond its originally intended functionality. The jewel case possesses specific transparent and opaque parts, which provide interesting lighting opportunities.

radial cd lamp shade for chandelier base bracket system on existing slots in standard jewel cases.

JO·2000

CD LAMP!

Blurred Focus
Adaptive Reuse

Temporal Graffiti

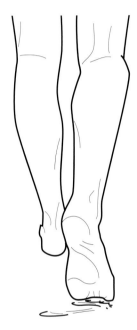

Mood Tray, Bar and Hose Lamp

Because of the pervasiveness of computing in our lives, surfaces are taking on dimensionality as never before. We will likely live to see every possible surface become a canvas for digital imagery. In 1995, as I began a design career, signposts indicated the shift from analog to digital surfaces. Curious about thermochromatic liquid crystals' ability to morph in reaction to temperature shifts by displaying spectral changes, I began to explore metaphors for this evolving terrain and to employ a design lens we might call temporal graffiti. Since the flat surfaces in our lives are modest opportunities for reflection, it seemed natural to consider them as candidates for this kind of temporal graffiti.

The mood tray evolved from a series of occasional tables I made while in graduate school. This product was shown in Milan as part of a product line with DMD, the original manufacturing arm of Droog Design, an avant-garde Dutch company.

Using this surface treatment on a service tray aligned an unspoken desire (the ability of a product to be a conversation piece) with an appropriate context. Because of the rapid heat exchange, the serving of coffee or tea lends itself to a target situation where such a transformation takes advantage of circumstances to produce the desired effect.

This investigation was pushed further in scale and context when I was invited in 1998 to design a bar for a restaurant in Philadelphia. This task took considerable engineering with the cooperation of a company that produced the liquid crystal material. At the time of its production, it was the largest such installation of its kind. This served as a remarkable sell point for the restaurant, as this action was cause for much discussion among its customers.

The temporal graffiti lens leading to a design solution manifested itself in what might be called mood lighting, in the case of the Hose Lamp. This experiment was driven largely by the development of a new kind of fiber optic cable, developed for specialty lighting applications where a high degree of side lighting was required.

This experimental object consists of a 10-meter length of flexible fiber optic cable with strong side-lighting capabilities wound onto a spring-loaded, industrial hose collector. A steel base accommodates a light box, which houses a metal-halide bulb and a motorized color wheel. Mounted toward the top of the hose collector is a box that houses two switches.

One turns the bulb on and off; the other engages a motorized, rotating color wheel enabling a repeating loop of spectral color changes for the hose. A sphere made of frosted, translucent resin is cast directly onto the end of the cable. It diffuses the intensity of the strong light emitted at the cable's terminus and has a hook that enables the hose to cling to an object or fixture.

Like the Tone Knob Lamp, the investigation here began with the idea that lighting could control atmospheric conditions and mitigate conflict between objects and their environment. The flexibility of the light-carrying cable plays a large role in this, as it can disseminate light as well as color where it is placed. This project appropriates the technology of the standard holiday rope light and directs it in a more powerful formal language to approximate the vocabulary of interior lighting.

The lamp's chassis incorporates its own strong projector lamp to send enough light through the optical cable to power 10 meters of the hose. Treating the cable as a retractable "shop hose" offered a compact and portable method for containing a huge length of deployable light. Like Picasso "drawing" in space using a hot poker with a glowing end to burn a line drawing into the negative of an overexposed image captured by *Life* magazine photographer Gjon Mili in 1949, this lamp allows one to customize a drawing in a space. While the Hose Lamp was built as a prototype only, it is now included in the permanent design collection of the Denver Art Museum and the corresponding publication US Design 1975-2000.

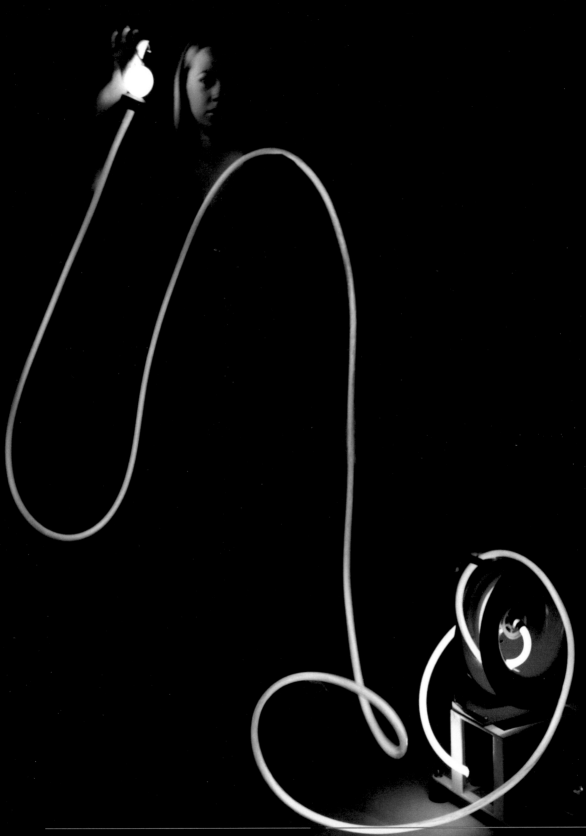

Blurred Focus
Temporal Graffiti

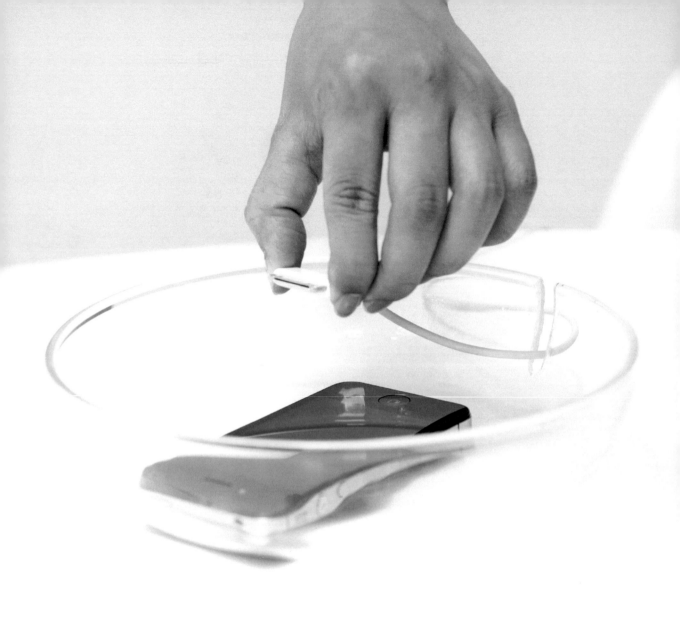

Alchemy

Prototypical Objects

The transformation of matter is the bread and butter of designers. Many designers apply a deep understanding of materials, technology, and technique at the core of moving ideas forward. This makes design an iterative process that requires seeing and testing in real time.

In fact, the promise of alchemy in general terms is that material metamorphosis could be rapid. In this regard, it's easy to point to 3D printing as an example. Yet no rapid prototyping is as instantly responsive to human control as the ancient techniques and processes controlled by hot-glass craft. Alchemy itself, a tool of design, is also a lens for seeing solutions.

I met the good people at the Corning Museum of Glass one summer after moving to Rochester. My wife and children took me to the Museum for a Father's Day visit, where we blew glass and wandered through the fascinating spaces, learning about the rich history of glass and the relative technologies and crafts associated with this singularly remarkable material. The Rakow Research Library at the Museum is the most extensive library on glass in the world. The resources of Corning are remarkable.

This reintroduction led quickly to some interdisciplinary projects for my students, colleagues, and professionals. To date, I've created conceptual projects with the Corning GlassLab in Rochester, Corning, and New York City, as well as at the Domaine du Boisbuchet in France.

I produced a body of work during an invited series of sessions known as GlassLab. I took advantage of this invitation to explore early-stage projects, like thoughts I wanted to explore—sketches in space. The GlassLab allowed me to make line drawings in space with volume and testable material characteristics. Working closely with the glassblowers made the translation from mind to matter possible with relative ease, with alchemy as a way to engage ideas as well as materials.

After two days of working together with master craftsmen at The Corning Museum of Glass, as a part of the GlassLab project, Tina Oldknow, former curator of modern glass, chose to accession three items from the sessions into the Museum's GlassLab prototype collection. The items consist of three functional vessels that address specific domestic conditions in the bedroom and bathroom.

The first item explores a tubeless approach to distributing toilet paper, by eliminating the typically wall-mounted roll-release system. Because the new toilet paper roll does not have a smooth internal cardboard component, it does not spin as easily and therefore raises the question, should it be deployed in the traditional manner at all? The answer is no. It turns out that deploying the tissue paper from the inside out actually works better. Therefore, when rethought as a floor piece, smooth deployment of the paper is uniquely possible.

The second item I envisioned was a shallow bowl to help manage bedside technology, such as smart phones. The idea was that if a bowl delineates the location for the technology, and perhaps also amplifies the sounds emanating from the device, it might have a simple intervention that also locates the charger, making it ready for use at all times and organizing behavior in this way.

The third project merges a toothbrush holder with a drinking cup to create efficiencies in often-cramped bathroom real estate, where the sink can prevent objects from sharing space. Here I also used the proximal lens, observing the intersection of basic physical needs: to dry a toothbrush after use and to rinse one's mouth out with water.

In all of these projects the alchemy lens helped me to rapidly test out ideas without the burden of refinement for use in the marketplace.

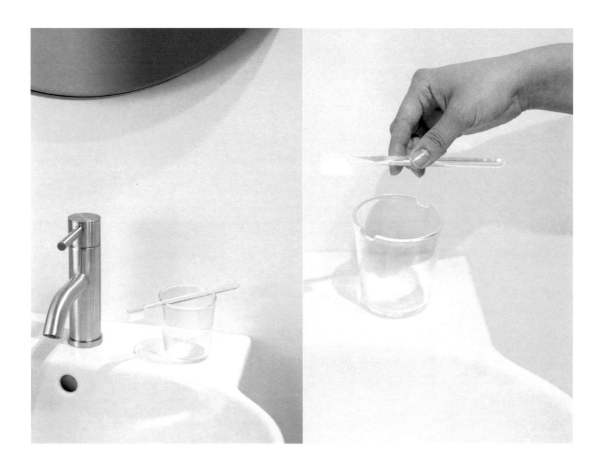

Deconstructed Lens

Taking things apart has long been a method for understanding how they go together in the first place and why. Having looked through the many lenses offered thus far, I felt that a final lens would be a meta-lens. In other words, a self-reflective and critical lens that observes how products are constructed in order to better contemplate their *raison d'etre*.

Cultural Resonance

SOS Stool for Casamania

The SOS stool blurs typological furniture boundaries. The two elements protruding from the seat can be used as cup or wineglass holders, handles, or hooks. The top surface features a rim and therefore offers the possibility to be used as a tray.

The SOS is included in the permanent design collections of Centre National d'Art et de Culture Georges Pompidou in Paris, the Philadelphia Museum of Art, the Musée des Beaux-arts de Montréal, and the Museum of the Rhode Island School of Design. Why would such an object engender this kind of cultural resonance?

Timeline

	2007									2008	
APR	MAY	JUN	JUL	AUG	SEPT	OCT	NOV	DEC	JAN	FEB

Josh Owen

APR	MAY	JUN	JUL	AUG	SEPT	OCT	NOV	DEC	JAN	FEB
Meeting with Casamania at Salone del Mobile in Milan, Italy					Working on initial models			Revisions begin		
		Research and concept ideation begin					Begin story development			

Casamania

APR	MAY	JUN	JUL	AUG	SEPT	OCT	NOV	DEC	JAN	FEB
				Meet in Italy to pitch concept Favorable responses		Working on first prototypes				
							Engineering begins			
								Tooling begins		

FEB	MAR	APR	MAY	JUN	JUL	AUG	SEPT	OCT	NOV	DEC

Photoshoot

Design Philadelphia planning begins

Print and electronic collatoral developed for product launch

Media Kits to domestic editors

Product debut in USA during Design Philadelphia

First publications appear in USA design journals magazines, blogs

First domestic sales in USA

Product launch at Salone del Mobile in Milan, Italy

Inducted into Pompidou Collection in Paris, France

Media Kits to international editors

First publications appear in European design journals, magazines, and blogs

European shipments

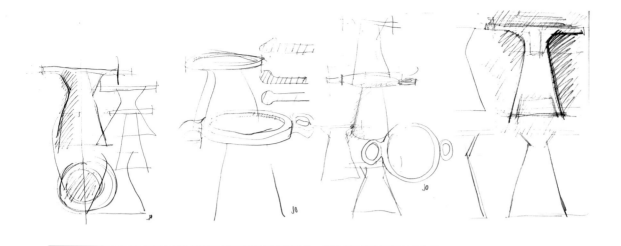

Stools are somewhat unusual within the lexicon of useful things because they lack a singular orientation. Without a back, a stool is not a chair. Therefore, a stool cannot offer significant, sustained ergonomic support. A stool can perform as a temporary seat, but it is not a bench; it has only room for one. It is a nomadic object. A stool has no specific or regularly programmed assignment within the context of a living room, kitchen, bedroom, or even waiting room, office, or poolside. However, it can be used in all of these places. It is compact and helpful at all costs. A good stool is transportable, durable, and only somewhat comfortable. It is at home both indoors and outdoors.

Casamania asked me to develop a suitable replacement for another rotationally molded polyethylene stool in its product line whose sales were waning. Finding a similar scale and price point was important to the bottom line of the project, as it would have to fit into this proven sales category.

The stool's position in the pantheon of furniture objects gives it an association with trays and occasional tables. These associations suggested that my stool should be similarly easy to carry, portable, and stackable. While designing this product, I sought physical stability and the potential for endurance.

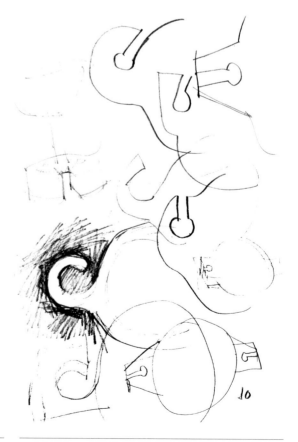

Mobility

Compactness

Durability

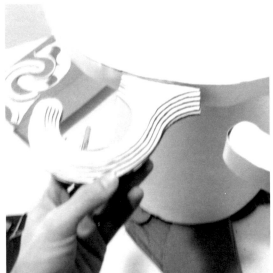

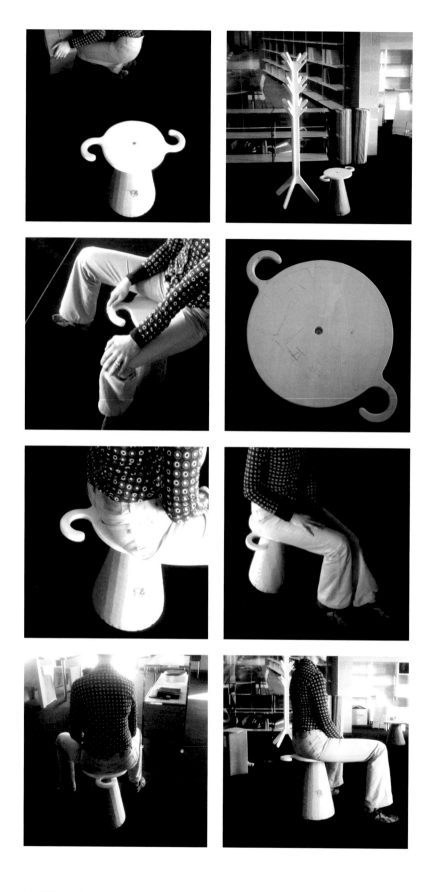

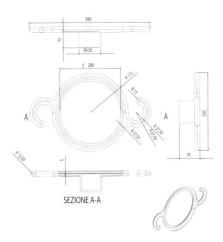

SEZIONE A-A

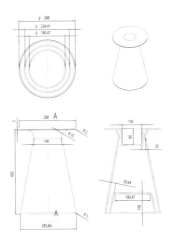

Once defined, the hook-like outriggers became handgrips that could hold stemware and cups. Stemware in particular engages well in the semantics of the broken circle by allowing for a larger circumference of base to pass through the hook when dropping in from above might be prohibitive. A subtle rim along the top or base of the seat provides a slight physical catch for items when in tray mode. This visual detail also plays an emotional role in projecting the promise of physical stability.

The naming of the project comports with the notion that the stool itself is a helper in situations of "distress." When one needs a boost, a temporary perch for objects, or for oneself, one reaches for a stool before a chair, table, or bench.

The global term SOS appealed because the product exists in a worldwide market. Also, using the lettering technique previously employed for the XX Coat Rack and XOX Coffee Table for Casamania lent itself naturally to this quite philosophically related product line.

Cultural resonance is exemplified by pushing the boundaries of a common object while retaining accessibility and universality in its design.

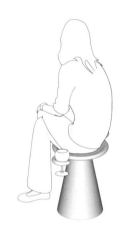

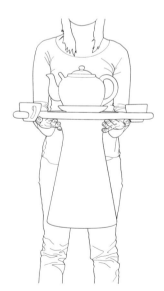

Deconstructed Lens
Cultural Resonance

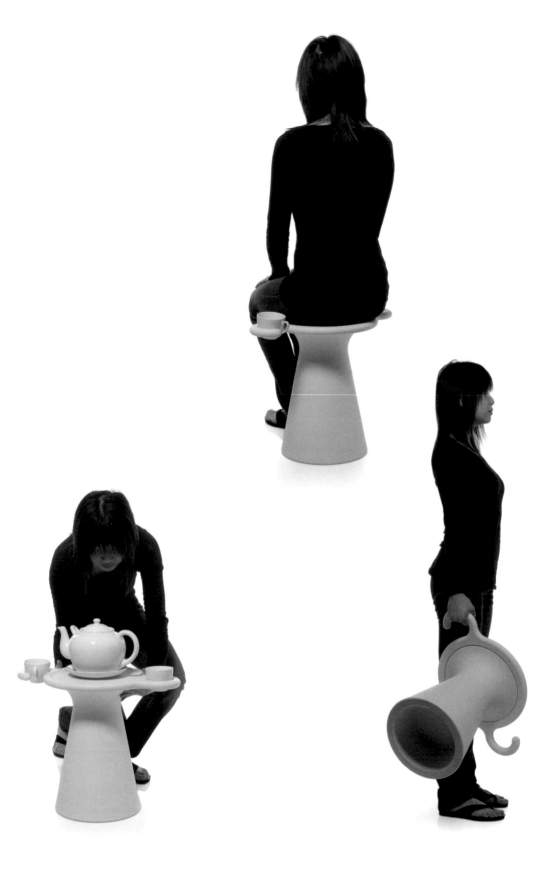

A Holistic Approach

8125 Calculator

The Monroe 8125 challenges the business strategy that a product should be engineered for obsolescence or that it should exist without a deep connection to the brand into which it fits. Understanding the history of Monroe helped me to take a holistic approach to rethinking their core product and reinvigorating the brand.

Timeline

	2005	2006					2007		
	SEPT	JAN	FEB	MAR	APR	MAY	JUN	JUL	AUG

Josh Owen

	2005	2006					2007		
	SEPT	JAN	FEB	MAR	APR	MAY	JUN	JUL	AUG
	Dialogue with Monroe company begins	Research begins		Conceptual development begins		Presentation of first concepts to Monroe	Dialogue resumes	Concept revisions	Presentation to Monroe

Monroe

	2005	2006					2007		
	SEPT	JAN	FEB	MAR	APR	MAY	JUN	JUL	AUG
	Dialogue with Josh Owen LLC begins					Presentation of first concepts	Dialogue resumes		Presentation of new concepts

	2008						2009				
	MAR	APR	MAY	JUN	SEPT	DEC	JAN	FEB	MAR	APR	MAY

MAR	JUN	SEPT	DEC	FEB	MAY
Dialogue reinitiated	Final Revisions	Revised Brand Identity	Manual and Packaging Design	Pre-production sample for Monroe evaluation	Product Photograpny
Conceptual development begins				Final Revisions to the Manual	
				Final Sample for Production Approval	

MAR	MAY	SEPT	DEC	MAR	APR
Dialogue reinitiated		Mock-up Sample of the calculator	Initial Tooling	Pre-production sample for evaluation	Final Sample for Production Approval
	Software Development begins		Software Development continues	Tooling Modification	

Monroe's loyal customers are accustomed to owning their products for a long time. They are also accustomed to a unique customer service experience that makes the operation, maintenance, and upkeep of Monroe products easy. The 8125 expands the functionality associated with previous Monroe models, while adding a reduced desktop footprint, improved overall usability, and a clear, rational form language for clarity and performance.

Taken from the 8125 User Manual:
About the 8125
Nearly a century has passed since Jay R. Monroe introduced the first commercial calculator to the business community. At the time, his vision was "to manufacture a machine to turn out routine figures; one that would add and subtract, multiply and divide with equal ease and would produce the answers almost as fast as they can be written down; that would be simple and practically foolproof to operate, with all factors used visible on the machine so the operator would know the answers were correct." "Such a machine," thought Monroe, "would greatly increase the efficiency of the office worker and would be a tremendous boon to the executive." While it would be hard to describe the first Monroe as "fast" by today's standards, it was certainly a huge advance, as all computations were performed manually at the time.

The Monroe 8125 is the beneficiary of that century of experience working directly with customers, some of the most enduring names in American industry. A Monroe sales representative has been in virtually every business, observing the accounting work routinely performed and providing feedback to Monroe's planning department for improvements in future products. Those improvements have always set the Monroe calculator apart from all others, as no other calculator company works directly with end users to simplify work routines.

The 8125 is an update to an established technology yet feels like a modern heirloom. This project is the result of a comprehensive brand program developed for Monroe that encompassed product, graphic, packaging, communication, and strategic brand management.

This project was fascinating to me because it was not a job to be shared with a general audience, but rather with a niche group of professional end users. This assignment demanded many technical requirements, including a powerful brand-affiliation that needed to be enhanced and enforced. The challenge was to analyze existing products and to look for efficiencies that could be leveraged to create a better version of similar, previous tools.

To do this, I was granted access to the company archives, where Monroe devices dating back to the first adding machines were available to inspect. The earliest of these devices, a product of necessity breeding clarity in engineering and graphic communication, interested me the most. Reductionist thought was not a fashion statement but rather, a brand identity. This is what I hoped to capitalize on in order to set the developmental plans in motion for the 8125.

In an effort to reduce parts-count, I re-thought the chassis of the device as a boat is designed: watertight hull with a deck above. This way, all parts dropped in from above, reducing the need for walls and a floor common in other units.

The paper-delivery system in prior units required metal components. Upon close inspection, I discovered that the paper roll would unfurl as efficiently without these added parts. I also discovered that a snap-fit canopy dust cover would be sufficient, and so designed that to be removable with one hand.

The functionalities in the keyboards were analyzed and reduced to the most important actions learned from a deep knowledge of user feedback provided by the company. The choice to keep the key design developed in prior models was another thoughtful decision based on the "touch" that loyal Monroe customers were used to. This is important, as users rely on the tactile feedback they receive from interacting with the keys when operating the machines at extremely high speeds. Varying design and engineering specifications affect such movements dramatically from company to company, with end users developing preferences that galvanize brand loyalty through performance.

 1920s

 1930–1940s

 1950s

 1958–1984

 1984–2001

MONROE *THE* CALCULATOR COMPANY 2001–Present

monroe Hyothetical Future

monroe

Readability is vitally important in the screen of the unit, so care was taken to spec a screen that was significantly larger than those typical to such units. I also took care to treat the manual, instructions, and labels with as much sensitivity as the other items, unifying even such mundane items as the battery replacement information molded onto the bottom of the chassis.

The issue of clarity in communication extends beyond the product into the packaging and the brand identity. Monroe agreed that in order to make a standout product, it would be critical to revisit the logo and standards the company had been using. So after a careful analysis of the history of Monroe's branding, I developed new standards and applications in order to celebrate heritage, maximize efficiencies, and produce an iconic look that was evocative of their position. My services, therefore, extended into the graphic design of the manual and packaging as well as the art direction of all photography that informed those components.

monroe 8125

monroe
the calculator company

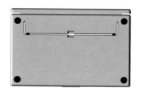

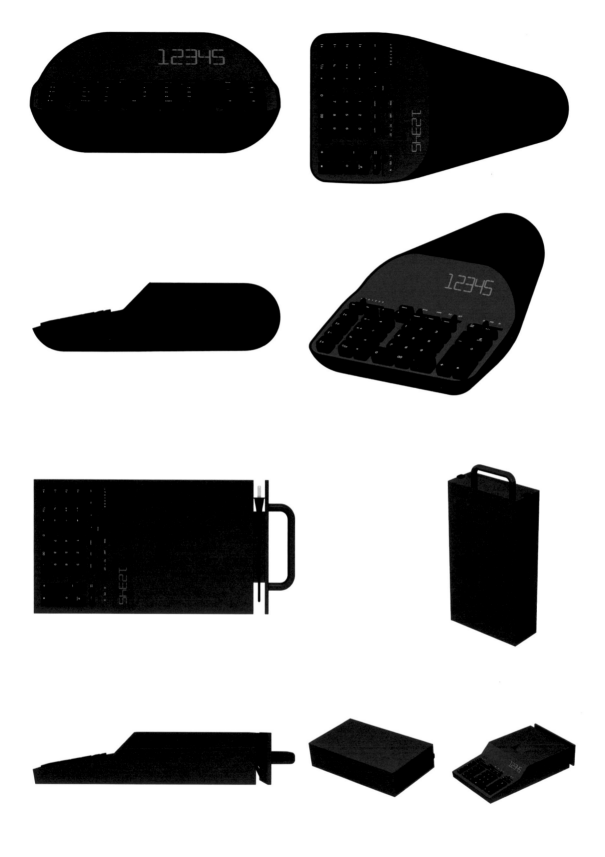

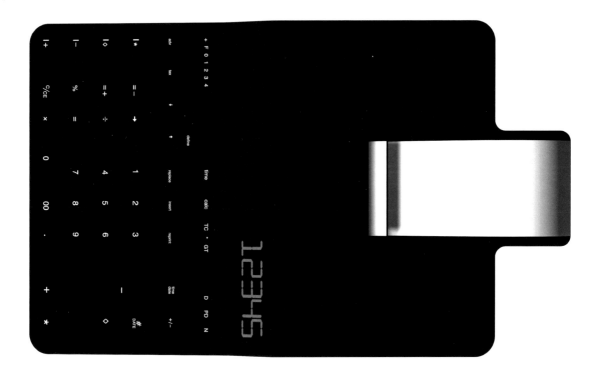

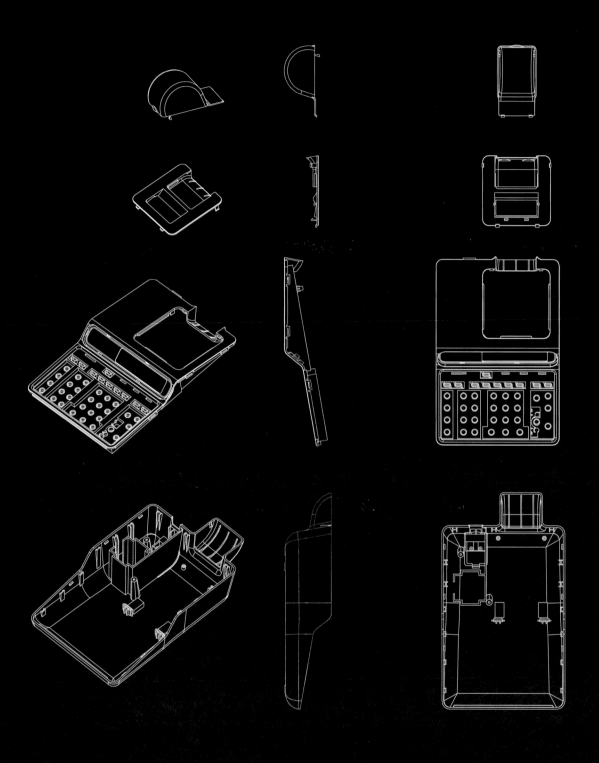

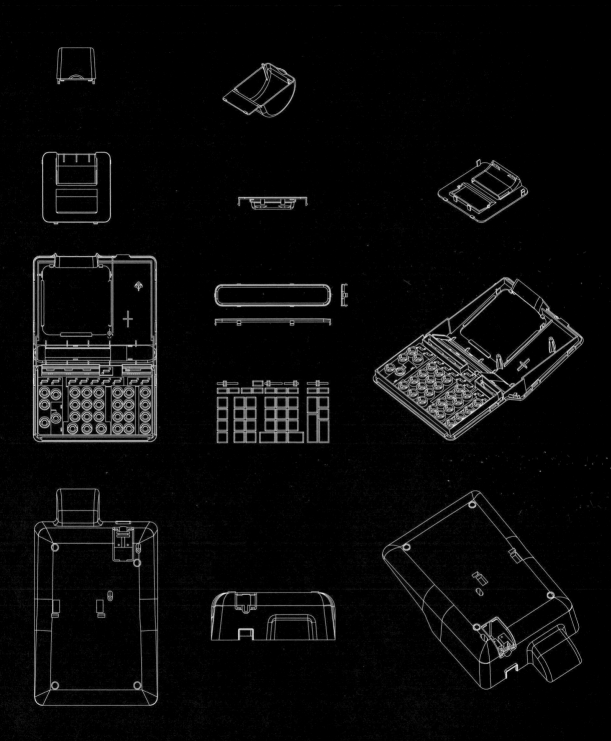

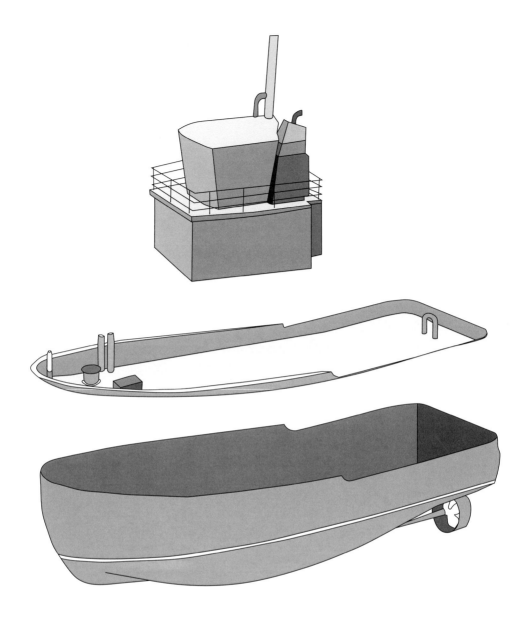
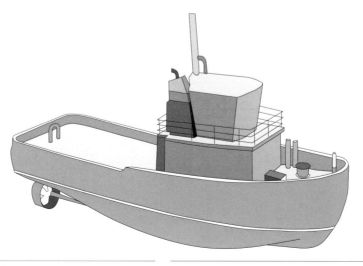

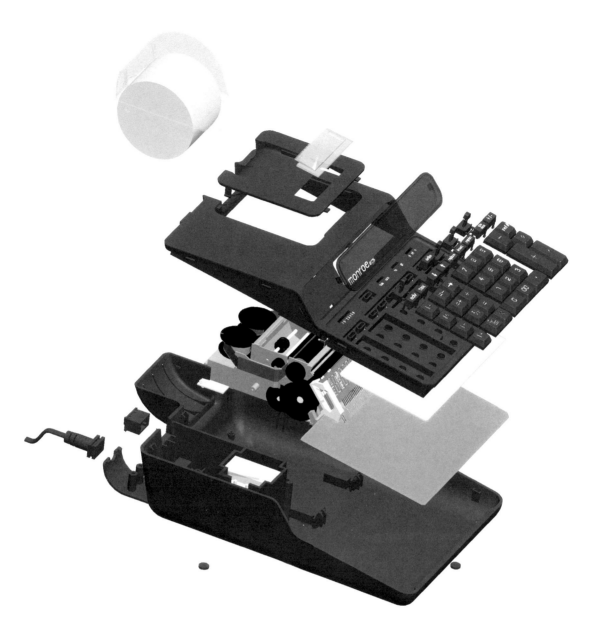

monroe
the calculator company

user manual

8125
desktop print display calculator
designed by josh owen

Product Family

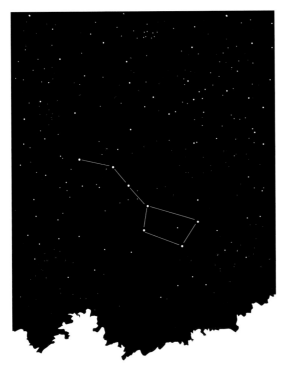

Constellation for Kontextür

Creating a constellation of objects for a company requires taking the license to develop multiple, related answers to design problems while paying attention to interrelated rituals, activities, and habits within a given environment. Such inquiry, and the possibility of consistency, can also broker loyalty in end users. Often, a singular material choice can dictate or enable such an investigation, as it did in the case of the Kontextür products.

Timeline

	2011					2012			
	JUN	JUL	AUG	OCT	NOV	JAN	FEB	APR	MAY

Tissue Box

JUN	JUL	AUG	OCT	NOV	JAN	FEB	APR	MAY
Research								
	Proto-typing	Factory samples		Packaging	Photography			Exhibited at Wanted Design in NYC
			Revisions					

WC Line

JUN	JUL	AUG	OCT	NOV	JAN	FEB	APR	MAY
	Research							
	Proto-typing		Factory samples	Packaging	WC line receives Chicago Atheneum Good Design Award			Exhibited at Wanted Design in NYC
			Revisions		Photography			

Hanging Line

JUN	JUL	AUG	OCT	NOV	JAN	FEB	APR	MAY
		Research						
		Proto-typing	Factory samples	Revisions	Photography			

Mirrors

JUN	JUL	AUG	OCT	NOV	JAN	FEB	APR	MAY
						Research	Proto-types	Factory samples

2012   2013

JUN   JUL   AUG   NOV   APR

Photoshoot

Photoshoot   WC Line exhibited
                                        at the Salone del
                                        Mobile, in Milan

Packaging   Photoshoot

          Revisions
                   Packaging
                   Photoshoot

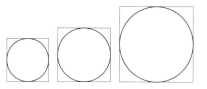

Circle vs Square

While my work with Kontextür began with a tissue box cover, the rationale for that product's success was highly dependent upon its relative context. The bathroom environment experiences dramatic shifts of temperature and humidity that demand suitable materials, often, traditionally, ceramic. Hard, stable, non-porous, but affordable, ceramic's drawback is its surface: too hard and too cold.

When you are most vulnerable—naked—which qualities do you prefer in your environment: hard and cold or soft and warm? The answer to this question led me to medical grade silicone, a durable, moldable, and flexible (displaying varying levels of rigidity) material. Because of its use in medicine, the material feels at home in the bathroom, where, I was able to begin imagining a landscape of uses.

The WC Line for Kontextür consists of a plunger with a storage dish, a toilet brush with a storage vessel, and a waste bin. The design for the WC Line uses functionality and performance as the primary measures to define beauty. These products, with their flexible materials, blend utility, usability, materiality, and engineering with careful attention to the concerns of bathroom space limitation. Based on circular footprints, these items relate to one another naturally in many configurations, never looking out of alignment in their settings. The wooden handles are sourced locally at the production site and the full silicone rubber construction is durable.

As with the other products I designed for Kontextür, one of the strategies in the design of the hanging mirrors was to ensure the long life of the products. By conceiving of the "holding" component of both mirrors as a glove to stretch over the glass, the mirror element is both contained and protected. Because the molded silicone is incredibly strong and tear resistant, if the mirror part is ever damaged or broken, it can be replaced by the consumer and re-fit into the proprietary design element. The wall-mounting system allows for precise placement without the extra step of measuring and marking the wall in advance of hanging. Holding the mirror in place shows exactly where it will hang when the screw is inserted. Like all the other items in the product family for Kontextür (with the exception of the hook) there are no extra parts trapped in the silicone, making recycling very easy, should that become desired.

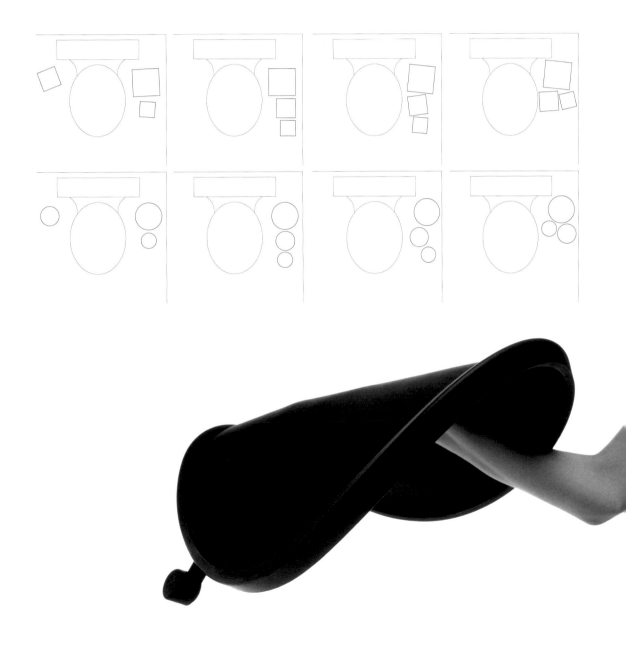

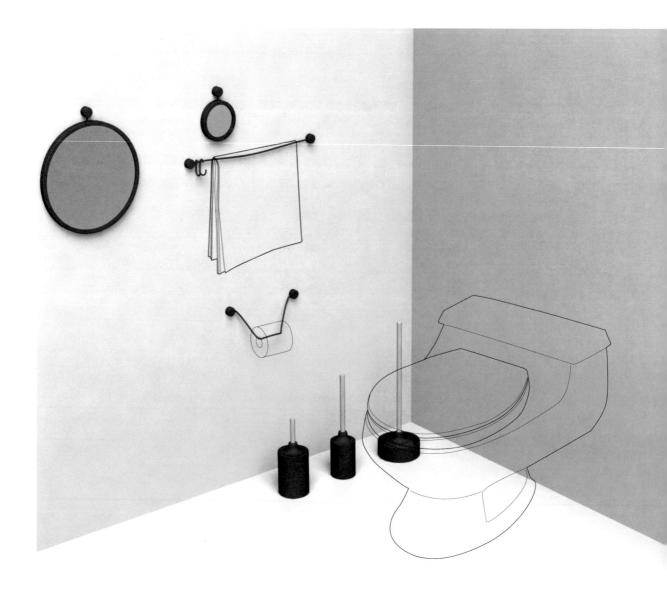

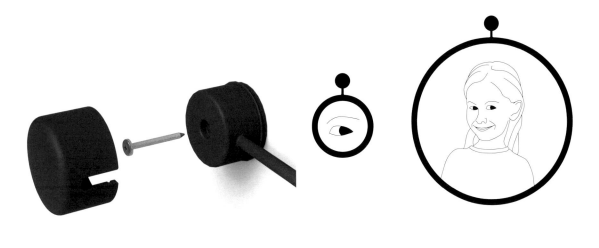

The Hanging Line consists of a wall mountable magazine/towel holder and a wall mountable toilet paper roll holder. The magazine/towel holder was developed to function as a minimalistic solution to the problem of storing reading material and towels in the bath. A special hook was also designed to accompany this system in order to provide extra utility for hand towels, bath tools, or reading glasses. The toilet paper holder uses a magnetic catch to quickly and intuitively interchange rolls with no removal of parts in the process.

Taken together, these items begin to address a contemporary vision for the bathroom, where details become softer, warmer, more flexible, and more enduring. Most importantly, the choices reflect a dialogue between objects and systems that speaks a consistent, clear, and common language of accessibility.

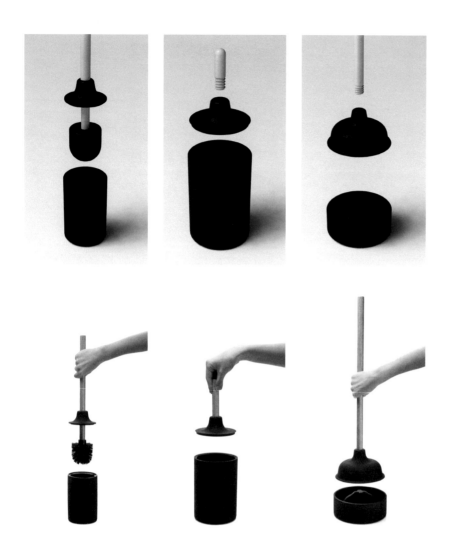

Deconstructed Lens
Product Family

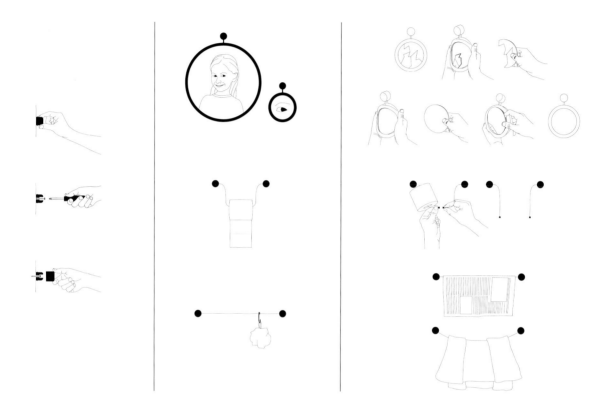

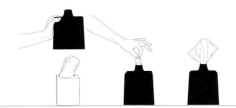

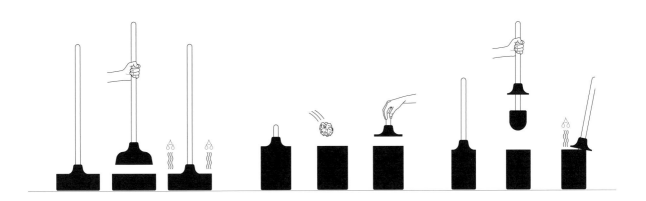

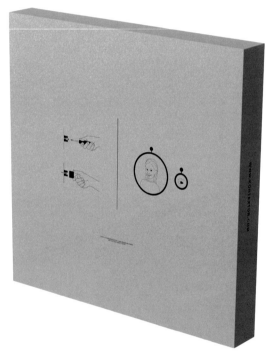

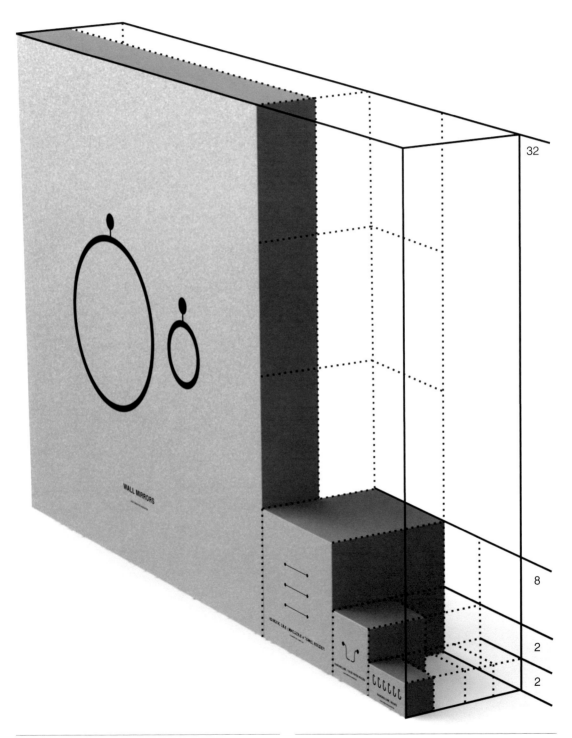

32

8

2

2

WALL MIRRORS

Deconstructed Lens
Product Family

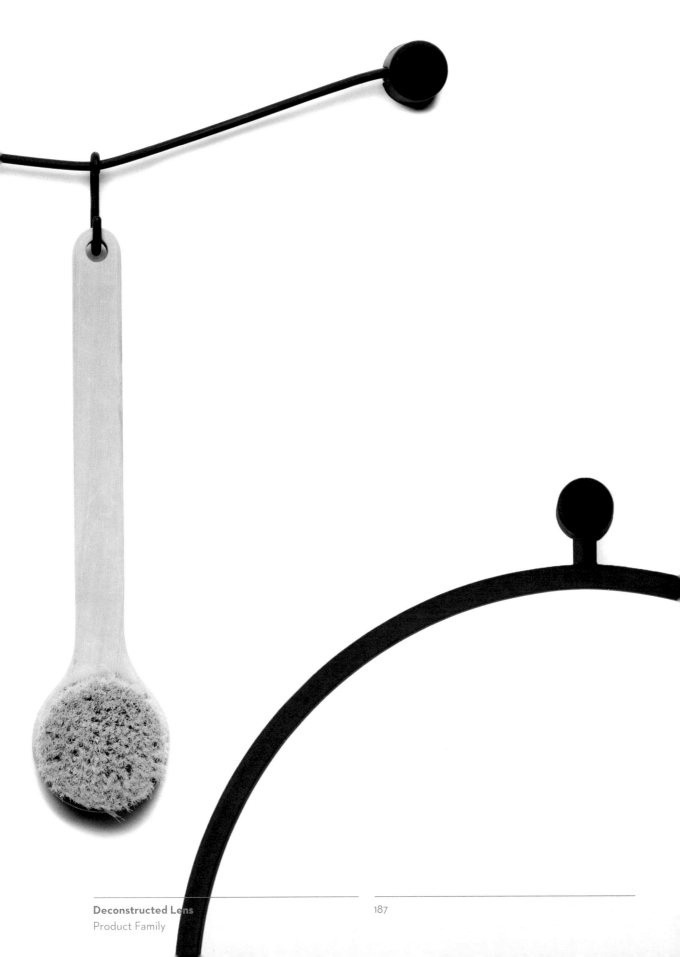

Deconstructed Lens
Product Family

Deconstructed Lens
Product Family

Universal Form

Kathryn B. Hiesinger

The J. Mahlon Buck, Jr. Family
Senior Curator of
European Decorative Arts
after 1700
Philadelphia Museum of Art

In an interview, Josh Owen said that his first paid design job was working as a freelancer in Aldo Rossi's New York studio, and I've always felt that in methodology and taste, he has never forgotten that training. Like Rossi and other Italian architects and designers of household objects in the last century, Owen follows the formal lessons of classical architecture. His aesthetic is based on pure, universal mathematical shapes—the circle being a favorite form—seen in his work at different scales, from the Tone Knob Lamp for Umbra (2001) and Chiaroscuro Clocks for Loll Designs (2013) to the XOX furniture he designed for Bozart (2003) and Casamania by Frezza (2006). At the same time, Josh is a functionalist designer, creating efficient objects whose use is evident from their form.

Josh's Italian forerunners were among the first to consider the sociocultural implications of product design. In recent years, such concern has been focused internationally on environmental issues. Josh Owen, too, has created products that use recycled materials, such as his Chiaroscuro Clocks made from standard milk jugs or his CD Chandelier (2001), a proposal that investigates the reuse of CD plastic cases and how their transparent and opaque surfaces can offer interesting lighting possibilities.

It is no accident that a number of his clients are Italian, among them Benza, Busso, and Casamania, who must recognize a sympathetic fellow traveler in Josh. His work is bold but refreshingly simple in appearance and uniquely his own in a period of diverse styles and influences. Using forms that are universal conceals how complex the technology, content, and meaning of his work can be or how carefully thought out their practical function is. In the end, Josh Owen uses his skills to solve design problems in imaginative ways, and that ability is essential in fulfilling his own stated objective of "designing, educating, and learning."

Normative Extremes

Nathaniel Popkin

Writer

Lately, I have been writing a novel about an architect who has lost faith in his profession. "Sustainability, materials, system efficiencies, form," he says. "Everything I do as an architect is based on ideas, notions, tastes, prevailing best practices someone else has figured out that are the same all across the world."

The architect wants to design buildings of authenticity that will matter in 10, 20, or 50 years, but he can't figure out how. What will possibly make his building matter?

Faced with a world that produces endless objects, and oceans of junk, industrial designers must often feel a similar sense of ennui and helplessness. The vast majority of "stuff" is unnecessary, inelegant, and toxic. Today, most technology seems intent on further separating the craftsman's hand from the manufacturing process.

Josh Owen may snarl from time to time at this state of affairs—and he must because it directly impacts his livelihood and sense of self—but his first great gift is his ability to focus and take delight in purity.

Above my desk I keep a quote from Italo Calvino's Invisible Cities. "And Polo said," begins the passage:

The inferno of the living is not something that will be; if there is one, it is what is already here, the inferno where we live every day, that we form by being together. There are two ways to escape suffering it. The first is easy for many: accept the inferno and become such a part of it that you can no longer see it. The second is risky and demands constant vigilance and apprehension: seek and learn to recognize who and what, in the midst of inferno, are not inferno, then make them endure, give them space.

When I read this, as I do each day, I think of Josh, who incidentally has spent months of time in Italy throughout his career. Indeed, in Venice, Marco Polo's city and the imaginative lens of Invisible Cities, I had the delight to witness the way Josh's work and his philosophy carve human space in the crush of city-as-commodity. (You can see my kids and Jasper Owen using Josh's SOS stool—clustered in the public areas of the 2009 Venice Biennale—to transform a corner of the Arsenale into a mini dining room on page 144.)

Beyond beauty, beyond even the purity of function, for Josh there is meaning. This is what guides his work and life, a continuous search for the essence of things. Notably for an artist who seeks essential truths, Josh is no fundamentalist. Meaning comes from the past, as he constantly pulls on the history of objects and artifacts in considering what modern humans could use, but also from the present, from the very way modern humans live. He is normative in the extreme.

But Josh employs normative analysis, which by nature is messy and fraught, in order to pare down concepts and to burn ideas into singular statements. In the midst of the inferno, Josh wants to know what's still standing. Nothing illustrates this better than Josh's distinct cast-iron Menorah, an object of functional and artistic perfection that he designed for Areaware in 2010.

When Josh lands on pure expression, as he does with the Menorah, his works speak to human beings as intelligent agents. There's no use in making something that doesn't prod the imagination... or feel good in the hand... or regale... or kid, he seems to say. In taking an object long lorded up with sloppy decoration and paring it down to pure form, Josh is also telling us why his work is so important, and what it means to be a designer in the paradoxical age of inferno and ennui.

Conclusion

Design as Lifestyle

The McGraw-Hill Dictionary of American Idioms and Phrasal Verbs defines "design as lifestyle" as "to do things with permanent effect; to be serious in one's actions." Looking out of an airplane window from 30,000 feet shows us humans to be similar to many other creatures in the way that our movements imprint on the planet, despite the general consensus that we are somehow different. Taking the long view on life and design can be a risky proposition. Yet as stewards of the planet, a broad perspective is quite important in order to frame complexities. Therefore, it is my sincere hope that applying design thinking to my own lifestyle has been a useful attempt at following my values as well as projecting them in order to promote them as exemplars.

One of the ways in which I have created efficiencies in my day-to-day life is by connecting living and working environments so that the physicality of my surroundings could promote healthier living and healthier working. Because my work is my passion, it is only natural that while somewhat separate, the spaces should be informed by close proximity.

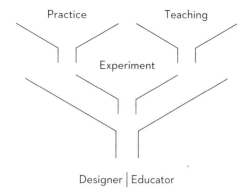

Practice   Teaching

Experiment

Designer | Educator

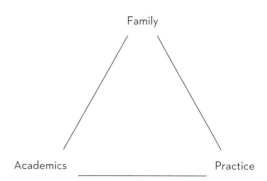

Family

Academics   Practice

My design studio has always been connected to my living spaces. When I began working as a young designer in Philadelphia, my wife and I rented an open plan, live-work space with little architectural delineation. This was not always ideal and led to the understanding that there should be permeable but separable physical boundaries.

When we purchased our first real estate, a section of a 1920s-era factory, we separated the spaces by a level. In that orientation, interns, mentees, and employees were able to come and go without passing through the living spaces. This new format favored combined living and working spaces with a clear division to support the need for privacy and family life; a strong addition and insight that proved to work well over time.

Studio	Home				University

After relocating our home and my studio to Rochester, NY, my wife and I purchased a building in a wooded lot in a village setting. The rural qualities of the context are conducive to both pleasurable living and focused working. The studio is an extension of residence, jutting outward into the woods on the property. The windows and skylights are designed to take advantage of a view of the surrounding trees and sky above. With all windows open, the studio is permeated by the sounds of birds and the wind in the trees. Windows are placed high along the walls above generous worktables, providing for pin-up space and focus without distraction of ground-level activities outside. A library is closely linked to the studio for reference. In designing the new studio, I created a compact and efficient workspace, free of the debris of most process and archival materials that are located in an adjacent workshop and another connected storage space for historical materials.

Having these two components of my life aligned has made for a streamlined process and workflow, key to managing the business of life and work and for promoting healthy productivity.

In order to decode these three aspects of my life and to show my progress, I have provided a timeline of my career delineated by personal milestones, academic accomplishments, and professional practice highlights.

Design is a lens through which I see the universe and an interconnected part of my physical and metaphysical well-being. It is not style or aesthetics, but a lifestyle choice born from a deep desire to craft the world from a humanistic standpoint.

And thus, everything I do is an act of design. I design my priorities, my house, my products, my clothes, my meals, my schedules, and my methods for teaching and communicating. If the results of this work emerge as beautiful, empathic, or effortless, this simply is the consequence of informed choices that emanate from a deep meditation on history, theory, and practice. Compelling design speaks for itself because the designer has done his job by making things better.

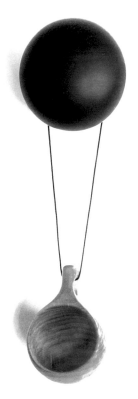

	1970	1974	1976	1988	1989	1994	1995	1996	1997	1998

Personal

	1970	1974	1976	1988	1989	1994	1995	1996	1997	1998
	Born Philadelphia, PA			Travels to Egypt, Greece Cyprus				Becomes engaged		Marries Marsha Wittink moves to Philadelphia
		Family moves to Ithaca, NY								
			Summers spent with father on archaeological excavations in Middle East		Begins playing guitar in rock band					

Academic

	1970	1974	1976	1988	1989	1994	1995	1996	1997	1998
				Attends Tel Aviv University		Artist in residence at Cornell		Attends RISD earns MFA in Furniture Design		
						Attends Cornell University earns BA in Visual Studies BFF in Sculpture studies in Rome, Italy			Teaches furniture course Moore College of Art	

Practice

	1970	1974	1976	1988	1989	1994	1995	1996	1997	1998
					Sells first sculpture			Work published for first time		Forms OwenLogik Design Graphic and Industrial Design Studio
						Records album with band Tours in New York				

1999	2000	2001	2002	2003	2004	2005	2006	2007	2008	2009

Son Jasper
born
First home
and studio

Daughter Saskia
born

Begins teaching
as Adjunct Professor
in Industrial Design
Philadelphia University

Manages
student design
competition
Philadelphia
Museum of Art

Collab

Build project
for ICFF

Begins as Lecturer
UPenn
Grad Archuitecture

Promoted to
Associate Professor
Philadelphia University
Becomes
Academic Coordinator
Study Abroad Program
Milan, Italy

Wilsonart
Project
Exhibition
in ICFF

Hired as full time
Assistant Professor
Industrial Design
Philadelphia University
Joins Collab

Publishes
first book
Big Ideas,
Small Packages
for Woodsphere

Begins
first major
commission for
manufacturer
Tone Lamp

Socks for
Soxbox
released

Flip Clip for Paris
Clocks for Benza
Magnito and Ashtray
for Kikkerland

Jigger
for Kikkerland

SOS Stool
for Casamania
Inducted into
Pompidou

Tone Lamp
for Umbria
released

Knockoff
Lamp, XOX table
for Bozart
Mood Tray for
Interior Tools

Stash, Big Ears
Flyswatter
for Kikkerland
Unbook
for Casamania

Doorstop
for Areaware

Calculator
for Monroe
Menorah
for Areaware

XOX Coffee
XX Coatrack
for Casamania

Timeline

	2009	2010	2011	2012

Personal

		2010		
		Accepts post at Rochester Institute of Technology		
		Relocates to Rochester, NY		

Academic

	2010	2011	2012
	Initiates Metaproject industry collaborations RIT series.	Initiates Product Timecapsule collection in Vignelli archives with Monroe 8125 calculator	Metaproject 03 with Areaware
	Metaproject 01 with Wilsonart International		GlassLab project added to CMoG permananet design collection
	Becomes an associate at Vignelli Center of Design Studies at RIT	Metaproject 02 with CMoG	
		Received tenure at RIT: becomes Chair of Industrial Design Program	

Practice

	2010	2011	2012
	Door Stopper in Chicago Atheneum permanent design collection	Menorah added to permanent design collection at National Museum of American Jewish History	Tissue Box cover for Kontextür	WC Line, Hanging Line, and Hanging Mirrors for Kontextür
	Initiates work on Lenses for Design book	SOS Stool added to permanent design collection at the Musée des Beaux Arts, Montreal	Menorah for Areaware in Chicago Atheneum permanent design collection	Perpetual Calendar for Busso

2013	2014	2015	2016

| GlassLab project added to CMoG permanent design collection | Metaproject 04 with Herman Miller

Promoted to Full Professor at RIT | Metaproject 05 with Kikkerland and Bed, Bath and Beyond | Metaproject 06 with Poppin wins Editor's Award at ICFF |

| WC Line in Chicago Atheneum permanent design collection

XX Coatrack added to Taiwan Design Museum permanent collection | SOS Stool added to RISD Museum permanent design collection

Clocks for Loll | Invited to run workshop at Boisbuchet, France

Begins final work on Lenses for Design book | Workshop with GlassLab at Domaine du Boisbuchet France

Spoon Set for Kikkerland | Perpetual Calendar at ICFF

Publishes Lenses for Design book |

Conclusion

215

Appendix

Products

2016	Spoon Set Designed for Kikkerland		2012	Waste Bin Designed for Kontextür
2014	Mailbox Designed for Loll		2011	Tissue Box Cover Designed for Kontextür
2013	Large Chiaroscuro Clock Designed for Loll		2010	Menorah Designed for Areaware
2013	Small Chiaroscuro Clock Designed for Loll		2009	8125 Calculator Designed for Monroe
2013	Perpetual Calendar Designed for Busso		2009	Hanging Door Stopper Designed for Areaware
2012	Large Hanging Mirror Designed for Kontextür		2008	Stoop Bench Designed for Dupont Corian
2012	Small Magnifying Mirror Designed for Kontextür		2008	sos Stool Designed for Casamania
2012	Magazine / Towel Holder Designed for Kontextür		2007	Aluminum Cube Jigger Designed for Kikkerland
2012	Toilet Paper Holder Designed for Kontextür		2006	Mini Magnito Salt + Pepper Designed for Kikkerland
2012	Hooks Designed for Kontextür		2006	Knock-off Lamp (reissued) Designed for Kikkerland
2012	Plunger Set Designed for Kontextür		2006	xx Coatrack Designed for Casamania
2012	Toilet Brush Set Designed for Kontextür		2006	xox Coffee Table Designed for Casamania

Products

2005	Magnetic Fly Swatter Designed for Kikkerland		2004	Six Socks Gift box set Designed for Conduit
2005	Unbook Coin Bank + Bookend Designed for Casamania		2003	Mood Tray Service Tray Designed for Interior Tools
2005	Big Ears Mini Corkscrew Designed for Kikkerland		2003	Knock-off Lamp Designed for Bozart
2005	Big Ears Bottle Stopper Designed for Kikkerland		2003	xox Table Designed for Bozart
2005	Stash Bottle Opener Designed for Kikkerland		2003	Moneypig Coin Bank Designed for Bozart
2004	Magnito Salt + Pepper Designed for Kikkerland		2002	Up Sock Designed for Soxbox
2004	Bookend Picture Frame Set Designed for Kikkerland		2002	Question Sock Designed for Soxbox
2004	Don't Ashtray Ashtray Designed for Kikkerland		2002	Odometer Sock Designed for Soxbox
2004	Doing Time Clock Designed for Benza		2002	Walk Sock Designed for Soxbox
2004	Time Flies Clock Designed for Benza		2002	98.6 Sock Designed for Soxbox
2004	Flip Clip Report Cover/binder Designed for Paris Business Products		2002	Wash Me Sock Designed for Soxbox
2004	Cheese Slicer Cutter Prototype		2002	Mercury Sock Designed for Soxbox

2002	Zipper Sock	
	Designed for Soxbox	
2001	CD Lamp	
	Prototype	
2001	Tone Knob Lamp	
	Designed for Umbra	
2001	Mood Bar	
	Installation	
1998	Two Part Chair	
	Prototype	
1997	Hose Lamp	
	Prototype	

Collections

2013	Museum of Congregation Emanu-El [3]
2013	Rhode Island School of Design Museum
2013	Taiwan Design Museum in Taipei
2012	Chicago Athenaeum
2012	Corning Museum of Glass [3]
2011	Chicago Athenaeum
2011	Vignelli Center for Design Studies
2010	Antiques of The Future
2010	Centre Pompidou
2010	Musee des beaux-arts de Montreal
2010	National Museum of American Jewish History
2009	Chicago Athenaeum
2008	Centre Pompidou
2008	Chicago Athenaeum
2008	Philadelphia Museum of Art
2007	Antiques of The Future [2]
2006	Chicago Athenaeum
2005	Chicago Athenaeum
2005	Museum of Modern Art Library Archives
2004	Antiques of The Future
2003	Antiques of The Future
2002	Denver Art Museum
2002	Museo Alessi
2001	Material Connexion

Awards

2015	Top Scholarship Contributor Award Rochester Institute of Technology
2014	Rank of Full Professor Rochester Institute of Technology
2012	Chicago Athenaeum Good Design Award
2012	Tenure at Rochester Institute of Technology
2011	Chicago Athenaeum Good Design
2011	Faculty Evaluation and Development Grant Rochester Institute of Technology
2009	Chicago Athenaeum Good Design
2009	Best of Philadelphia Award
2008	Chicago Athenaeum Good Design
2008	Best of Philadelphia Award
2008	Craig R. Benson Chair for Innovation
2008	Red Dot Design Award, Honorable Mention
2007	International Design Awards, First Place Winner
2007	ICFF Design School Entry
2006	Mathmos 'Candle Light' Competition, Finalist
2006	ID Annual Design Review, Honorable Mention
2006	Designboom House Party Competition, Finalist
2006	Chicago Athenaeum Good Design
2005	MACEF Design Award: Rethink + Recycle, Finalist
2005	Brooklyn Museum Young Designer Award, Nominee
2005	Athena Emerging Designer Award, Nominee
2005	ICFF Editors Award
2005	ID Annual Design Review, Honorable Mention
2005	Chicago Athenaeum Good Design
2005	Surface Designing The Future, Runner-up

2004	Spertus Museum Award, Second Place
2003	Graphis Product 3
2003	Philadelphia Magazine Award: 22 People
2003	Surface Ten Avant-Garde Designers,
2003	Smithsonian Smart Paper Kite Competition, Finalist
2000	Spertus Museum Award, Finalist
1998	Chrysler Award for Innovation In Design, Nominee
1997	Samuel Gragg Award for Achievement,
1993	Michael Rapuano Design Award
1993	Cornell University CCA Grant
1992	David Bean Traveling Artist Scholarship

Exhibitions

2015	Casamania Salone del Mobile Rho Fiera, Milan, ITALY
2015	Ambiente 2015: USA Partner Country Messe Frankfurt Exhibition Fairgrounds, Frankfurt, GERMANY
2014	Crafting the Cocktail Craft in America Center Los Angeles, CA, UNITED STATES
2014	Loll Designs + RIT Wanted Design New York, NY, UNITED STATES
2013	Traditional By Conception, Modern By Design: Museum of Congregation Emanu-El San Francisco, CA, UNITED STATES
2013	Loll Designs International Contemporary Furniture Fair, Jacob Javits Center New York, NY, UNITED STATES
2013	Loll Designs Wanted Design New York, NY UNITED STATES
2013	Risk and Certainty in Uncertain Times Wanted Design New York, NY, UNITED STATES
2013	Risk and Certainty in Uncertain Times Ventura Lambrate Milan, ITALY

Exhibitions

2013	The Next Wave: Industrial Design Innovation in the 21st Century Artisphere Washington, DC, UNITED STATES
2013	Art Reflected The Memorial Art Gallery Rochester, NY, UNITED STATES
2012	Four Corners: Design from Philly surrounds Minima gallery Philadelphia, PA, UNITED STATES
2012	Kontextür Wanted Design New York, NY, UNITED STATES
2012	Glass Lab The Corning Museum of Glass Corning, NY, UNITED STATES
2012	Areaware International Contemporary Furniture Fair, Jacob Javits Center New York, NY, UNITED STATES
2012	Kikkerland International Contemporary Furniture Fair, Jacob Javits Center New York, NY, UNITED STATES
2012	Do Not Destroy: Trees, Art, and Jewish Thought Contemporary Jewish Museum San Francisco, CA, UNITED STATES
2011	UMUL 2011 Hands On Milano Design Week Universita Cattolica di Milano, Milan, ITALY
2011	Casamania Salone del Mobile Rho Fiera, Milan, ITALY
2011	Areaware International Contemporary Furniture Fair, Jacob Javits Center New York, NY, UNITED STATES
2010	American Design in Paris Triode Design Showroom Paris, FRANCE
2010	Areaware International Contemporary Furniture Fair, Jacob Javits Center New York, NY, UNITED STATES
2010	Good Design Show: The World's Leading Design Chicago Athenaeum Chicago, IL, UNITED STATES
2010	Japan Media Arts Festival Pera Museum Istanbul, TURKEY
2009	Dorothy Saxe Invitational Exhibition The Contemporary Jewish Museum San Francisco, CA, UNITED STATES

2009 Dupont Corian Bench Invitational for Design
Philadelphia
Schuylkill River Banks
Philadelphia, PA, UNITED STATES

2009 Objective Affection
Boffo NYC
New York, NY, UNITED STATES

2009 Eco-Logical Thinking: Products for the Next
Generation
The Chelsea Art Museum
New York, NY, UNITED STATES

2009 Areaware
International Contemporary Furniture Fair,
Jacob Javits Center
New York, NY, UNITED STATES

2009 Bowl Project Invitational
The Philadelphia Art Alliance
Philadelphia, PA, UNITED STATES

2008 Good Design, Small Things
Dieu Donne Gallery
New York, NY, UNITED STATES

2008 Biennale of Architecture
The Park Giardini
Venice, ITALY

2008 Design Philadelphia
DWR Showroom
Philadelphia, PA, UNITED STATES

2008 Deceptive Design: Experiments in Furniture
Chicago Cultural Center
Chicago, IL, UNITED STATES

2008 Kikkerland
International Contemporary Furniture Fair,
Jacob Javits Center
New York, NY, UNITED STATES

2008 Casamania, Salone del Mobile
Rho Fiera
Milan, ITALY

2007 Kikkerland Celebrates 15 Years of Design in
NYC
MXYPLYZYK Showroom
New York, NY, UNITED STATES

2007 Josh Owen + Surface Magazine for Art Basil
Sisley Shop with Belvedere and Kikkerland
Miami, FL, UNITED STATES

2007 Casamania, Salone del Mobile
Rho Fiera
Milan, ITALY

2007 Josh Owen + Casamania @ OLC for Design
Philadelphia
OLC Showroom
Philadelphia, PA, UNITED STATES

2006 Designboom Design Mart Invitational, ICFF
Jacob Javits Center
New York, NY, UNITED STATES

Exhibitions

2006   Designboom House Party Exhibition, 100%
         Design Tokyo
         Jingu-gaien Fairgrounds
         Tokyo, JAPAN

2006   Mathmos Candlelight Exhibition, 100% East
         (100% Design)
         Truman Brewery
         London, UNITED KINGDOM

2006   Fosters' Fosters Josh Owen for Design
         Philadelphia
         Fosters Urban Homeware Showroom
         Philadelphia, PA, UNITED STATES

2006   Pitti Living / Exhibition of New Projects
         Via Tortona 58
         Milan, ITALY

2006   Casamania of New Projects
         15 Corso Monforte
         Milan, ITALY

2006   Casamania, Salone del Mobile
         Rho Fiera
         Milan, ITALY

2006   Museum of Architecture and Design annual
         GOOD DESIGN Exhibition
         The Chicago Athenaeum
         Chicago, IL, UNITED STATES

2005   Designboom Design Mart Invitational, ICFF
         Jacob Javits Center
         New York, NY, UNITED STATES

2005   Random Access Memory: Group exhibition
         of designer's work-spaces from around
         the world
         Istanbul Design Week
         Istanbul, TURKEY

2005   Emergent: New Directions in Sustainable Art
         and Design
         Rhode Island School of Design
         Providence, RI, UNITED STATES

2005   Random Access Memory: Group Exhibition
         of designer's work-spaces from around the
         world
         Matatu Gallery
         Milan, ITALY

2005   Avant-garde Industrial: A selection of
         cutting edge product design from
         Philadelphia-based designers
         Philadelphia International Airport
         Philadelphia, PA, UNITED STATES

2005   Casamania, Salone del Mobile
         Milan Fairgrounds
         Milan, ITALY

2005   Josh Owen: Big Ideas / Small Packages
         222 Gallery
         Philadelphia, PA, UNITED STATES

2004   Conduit Group Exhibition
         Felissimo Design House
         New York, NY, UNITED STATES

2004   Eternal Flame: The 2004 Philip & Sylvia
        Spertus Judaica Prize Competition Exhibition
        Spertus Museum
        Chicago, IL, UNITED STATES

2003   Conduit Group Exhibition
        Lyonswier Gallery
        New York, NY, UNITED STATES

2003   US Design: 1975-2000
        Memphis Books Museum of Art
        Memphis, TN, UNITED STATES

2003   Genius Jones: Group Exhibition of Bozart
        Artists
        Miami Design District
        Miami, FL, UNITED STATES

2003   Surface TAG (Ten Avant-Garde) Industrial
        Design Showcase NYC
        Chelsea Art Museum
        New York, NY, UNITED STATES

2003   Playthings: The Fun Side of Design
        San Francisco Design Museum
        San Francisco, CA, UNITED STATES

2003   US Design: 1975-2000
        Museum of Arts & Design
        New York, NY, UNITED STATES

2003   Surface TAG (Ten Avant-Garde) Industrial
        Design Showcase NYC
        Jacob Javits Center
        New York, NY, UNITED STATES

2003   Smart Paper Kite Exhibition
        Smithsonian Arts & Industries Building
        Washington, DC, UNITED STATES

2003   Simple & Direct; An Investigation in
        Furniture Design
        The Design Center at Philadelphia University
        Philadelphia, PA, UNITED STATES

2003   Surface TAG (Ten Avant-Garde) ID
        Showcase Milano
        Salone del Mobile
        Milan, ITALY

2003   Interior Tools
        Salone del Mobile
        Milan, ITALY

2002   Soxbox Window + Release Party
        Fosters Urban Homeware Showroom
        Philadelphia, PA, UNITED STATES

2002   What Is Design Today?
        The Design Center at Philadelphia University
        Philadelphia, PA, UNITED STATES

2002   Recent Projects from
        The Owenlogik Design Lab
        Koussevitzky Gallery
        Pittsfield, MA, UNITED STATES

2002   US Design: 1975-2000
        Denver Art Museum
        Denver, CO, UNITED STATES

Exhibitions

2001	Innovative Products Exhibition Product Innovation Gallery The Material Connexion New York, NY, UNITED STATES
2001	The Logik of Josh Owen In Rare Form Gallery Lambertville, NJ, UNITED STATES
2000	Abitare il Tempo: Beyond European Design Projects From Around The World Verona, ITALY
2000	Torah Cover: The 2000 Philip & Sylvia Spertus Judaica Prize Competition Exhibition Spertus Museum Chicago, IL, UNITED STATES
2000	Philadelphia Designs Exhibition City Hall Philadelphia, PA, UNITED STATES
2000	2000 Objects for the New Millennium Exhibition Gallery 91 New York, NY, UNITED STATES
2000	New Frontiers In Furniture & Lighting Paley Design Center Philadelphia, PA, UNITED STATES
2000	Lights-ON: New ideas in lighting Jon Elder Gallery New York, NY, UNITED STATES
1999	Mr. Prototype: A Show of Industrial Design & Innovation Harry Allen Studio Showroom New York, NY, UNITED STATES
1998	New Materials Exhibition, Material Innovation Gallery Material Connexion New York, NY, UNITED STATES
1997	Materialistic, ID Gallery Rhode Island School of Design Providence, RI, UNITED STATES
1997	Salon du Meuble Le Bourget Paris, FRANCE
1997	Nine Artists, Herbert F. Johnson Museum of Art Cornell University Ithaca, NY, UNITED STATES

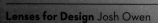

Acknowledgments

To my wife and collaborator in life, Marsha, this book could not have been possible without your love, encouragement, and perspective. We often say that your work as a physician is to make people better, while my work as a designer is to make things better. But the truth is that making people better cannot be disengaged from making things better, because the two are inseparable, like us. Giving people useful and meaningful tools to live fuller and more connected lives is as much the job of a physician as it is a designer. Thank you for being a constant reminder of this truth.

To my partners in industry: Because of your visionary collaboration, I have had the privilege to bring together culture and commerce in many meaningful ways. Together we have the power to make a positive impact on the world. Among many others, a special thanks to Noel Wiggins and Lisa Yashon and your teams at Areaware; Giovanni Pellone and your team at Benza; Larry Mangel and your team at Bozart; Elis Doimo, Loris Tessaro and Natascia Tesser and your team at Casamania; Rob Cassetti, Steve Gibbs, Eric Meek and Tina Oldknow at The Corning Museum of Glass; Jan Van der Lande, Laura Kellner, Perrine Giacomazzo and Jay Lee at Kikkerland; Kenneth Schiller at Kontextür; Greg Benson, Jeff Taly and Nate Heydt at Loll Designs; Dick Roberts at Monroe; Gerry Toscani and your team at Paris Business Products and Les Mandelbaum, Paul Rowan and your teams at Umbra.

To my studio interns, mentees and employees, past and present, I have you all to thank for helping me move my many projects forward. Designing a book has not been a linear process, nor has it been the target of my constant attention—making it even less linear. It has, however, been of great importance to me over the years and you have all encouraged and contributed in a variety of ways. In particular, I offer my thanks to Chris Ineson, who began the work of this book with me in 2009. Thank you to Flora and David Strauss, who helped further its implementation during the summer of 2013. Thank you, Jeff Sprague and Jane Lim, who pushed it to the next level with me in the summer of 2015. And thank you, Veronica Lin, who helped get it to the printer in 2016.

To my friend, colleague, and comrade, RIT Professor Bruce Ian Meader, your wisdom and vision for the design of this book is as clear and precise as your mind. Your attention to detail is matched only by your good cheer and deep commitment to thoughtful communication design. I have the greatest admiration for you, amigo.

To my friend N. R. Popkin, who stepped in during the 11th hour with editorial help. You are family. Thank you for your belief in my contribution to humanity.

To RIT Provost Jeremy Haefner, former RIT School of Design Administrative Chair Patti LaChance, and RIT Professor Stan Rickel, thank you all for your honorable efforts in recruiting me to RIT. I would not have come without each of your personal contributions and persistence to that long conversation. Joining RIT has ranked among the best decisions of my life.

To RIT Professor Roger Remington, thank you for your friendship, mentorship, and partnership in the Vignelli Center for Design Studies, and beyond. I feel extremely fortunate to have had the opportunity to work so closely with such an important figure in the world of design education. You've taught me much and I look forward to much more. As you say, "Onward."

To RIT [College of Imaging Arts & Sciences] Dean Lorraine Justice and Administrative Chair of the School of Design, Peter Byrne, thank you both for your enthusiastic support, guidance, and partnership in leadership at RIT. I feel humbled to be a part of a significant moment in the life of our institution that falls under your stewardship.

To the contributing writers Kathryn B. Hiesinger, Scott Klinker, Nathaniel Popkin, Mathias Schwartz-Clauss, and the photographers Clint Blowers, Elizabeth Lamark and her team, Critter Knutsen and Julie Marquart, whose words and images fill this book, thank you all for adding the depth of informed outside perspective to frame the context of my efforts.

To my colleagues in Industrial Design and other collaborative disciplines at RIT, Philadelphia University, and the University of Pennsylvania, thank you all for the friendship, mentorship, and collegiality over the years. And thank you all for valuing professional practice within design education.

To the RIT Press, Bruce Austin, Molly Cort, Laura DiPonzio Heise, and Marnie Soom, cheers!

To my family, it should go without saying that your love and support makes life a joyful process. Thank you for everything.

Photo Credits

Elizabeth Lamark

2, 6, 8, 10, 12, 16, 17, 20 (RIGHT), 21 (BOTTOM), 24, 40, 42 (BOTTOM), 43, 44, 45 (TOP), 46, 64, 66, 68, 82, 83, 88, 89, 94, 96, 98 (TOP RIGHT), 104, 106, 107, 112, 126, 129, 130, 166, 170, 175 (BOTTOM), 178 (CENTER, BOTTOM LEFT), 179 (BOTTOM), 184, 185, 186, 187, 188, 189, 198, 199, 200, 201, 202, 203, 204, 205, 206, 207, 208, 209, 210, 211

Clint Blowers

4, 26, 28 (LEFT), 29, 30, 31, 32, 34 (RIGHT), 36, 39 (BOTTOM), 48, 51, 52, 54 (RIGHT), 55 (LEFT), 70, 72, 74, 75, 76, 77, 78, 80 (RIGHT), 81, 84, 86 (BOTTOM), 87 (TOP, BOTTOM RIGHT), 90, 92 (RIGHT), 93 (TOP), 99, 100, 102 (RIGHT), 103 (RIGHT) 108, 110, 111, 114, 116, 117 (RIGHT), 118, 120 (TOP), 121, 132, 146, 147, 148, 165, 167, 168, 169

Josh Owen LLC

9, 11, 15, 18, 19, 21 (TOP), 22, 27, 28 (RIGHT), 33, 34 (LEFT) 35, 37, 38, 39 (TOP), 41, 42 (TOP), 45 (BOTTOM), 49, 50, 53, 54 (LEFT), 55 (RIGHT), 57, 58, 59 (TOP), 61, 62 (BOTTOM), 65, 67, 71, 73, 79, 80 (LEFT), 85, 86 (TOP), 87 (BOTTOM LEFT), 91, 92, 93 (BOTTOM), 97, 98 (TOP LEFT, BOTTOM), 101, 102 (LEFT), 103 (LEFT), 105, 109, 115, 117 (LEFT), 119 120 (BOTTOM), 123, 124 (RIGHT) 127, 128, 133, 136, 137, 138, 139, 140, 141, 142, 143, 144, 145 149, 152, 153, 154, 155, 156, 157, 158, 159, 160, 161, 162, 163 164, 171, 174, 175 (TOP), 176, 177, 178 (TOP, BOTTOM RIGHT) 179 (TOP), 180, 181, 182, 183, 196, 197, 228

Critter Knutsen

56, 59 (BOTTOM), 60, 62 (TOP), 63, 122

Julie Marquart

124 (LEFT), 125

Corning

20 (LEFT), Courtesy of the Corning Incorporated Department of Archives & Records Management, Corning, NY

David Owen

14

Index

Colophon

Edited by Molly Q. Cort

Production by Marnie Soom

Designed by Bruce Ian Meader and Josh Owen

Typefaces are Helvetica designed by Max Miedinger
with input from Eduard Hoffmann
and Neutraface 2 Text designed by Christian Schwartz
inspired by architect Richard Neutra's
dimensional number designs
assisted by Richard Neutra's son Dion Neutra

Printed on McCoy Silk Text 100-pound text

Printing and binding by Jostens Book Manufacturing
Clarksville, Tennessee, USA

RIT Press acknowledges
the support for publication of this book
provided by
Jeremy Haefner, Senior Vice President
for Academic Affairs and Provost
and by Lorraine Justice, Dean
College of Imaging Arts and Sciences
Rochester Institute of Technology